# UNCOMMON BELIEFS

STEPHEN MACKEY
*WALL STREET JOURNAL* Bestselling Author

# UNCOMMON BELIEFS

## SEVEN PRINCIPLES TO BUILD A COMPETITIVE EDGE THAT LASTS

WILEY

Published by John Wiley & Sons, Inc., Hoboken, New Jersey.



***Library of Congress Cataloging-in-Publication Data:***

Names: Mackey, Stephen (Development coach) author
Title: Uncommon beliefs : seven principles to build a competitive edge that lasts / Stephen Mackey.
Description: Hoboken, New Jersey : John Wiley & Sons, Inc, [2027] | Includes index.
Identifiers: LCCN 2026027528 (print) | ISBN 9781394431595 cloth | ISBN 9781394431618 adobe pdf | ISBN 9781394431601 epub
Subjects: LCSH: Leadership | Leadership—Psychological aspects | Executive coaching | Career development
Classification: LCC HD57.7 .M33435 2027 (print) | LCC HD57.7 (ebook)
LC record available at https://lccn.loc.gov/2026027528
LC ebook record available at https://lccn.loc.gov/2026027529

Cover Design: Wiley
Author Photo: Teressa Jane Photography

Printed and bound by CPI Group (UK) Ltd, Croydon, CR0 4YY

C9781394431595_050926

# Contents

# When Talent Isn't Enough

I need to tell you about Diana Davis and Lisa Gorzyski.

It was seventh grade, and I had a foolproof, completely reasonable, entirely realistic plan to ensure that Diana Davis and Lisa Gorzyski would know that I existed. The plan was simple: I was going to play football, be the biggest, strongest dude on the team, and by the end of the week, the ladies would know and love me.

And for one glorious afternoon, the plan seemed to be working.

It was the first day of football practice, and the energy and excitement were off the charts. The drills were intense—man on man, bull in the ring, big on big—and I was absolutely destroying people. I knew, beyond a shadow of a doubt, that my plan was going to work.

Life was good . . . until it wasn't.

I discovered the first problem with my plan when my coach blew his whistle and said four words that would strike fear into the hearts of big men everywhere: "Get on the line."

It was time to run sprints.

This may not come as a surprise to you, but it was the shock of the century to me. Until that moment, I did not know that you had to run sprints to play football. Call me naive. Call me uninformed. But the reality is that I was not built for sprints. I was far from the paragon of bearded masculinity that I am today.

I was what the department stores called *husky*. My mother called me *big-boned*. My favorite food was a Twinkie.

So when my coach said get on the line for sprints, I had a very simple response: hard pass.

"I don't need to run to play football," I thought. "I just need to be bigger than everybody else. And I have that on lock."

But my coach looked at me and gave me a choice: Get on the line or take your helmet off and quit.

I took my helmet off and quit.

And just like that, my foolproof plan made me a fool.

What you need to know about that moment—what makes it more than a funny story and important to the genesis of this book—is this: When I stepped off that field, I took a step toward becoming the failure many people said I would be.

I am biracial. I was born to a white teenage mother, and a black biological father I would not know for most of my life, in a small Texas town where racism was far from gone. Statistically speaking, the odds were stacked against me. The numbers said I was less likely to graduate high school, less likely to attend college, more likely to be arrested before adulthood, and more likely to spend my life in poverty.

The statistics said I would be a failure.

And that day, I took a step toward proving them right.

■ ■ ■

The year that followed seventh grade was the worst of my life. I had no direction, no purpose, and no meaning.

Everything I thought would be my advantage had disappeared. And I was left with a question I didn't know how to answer: Is there not more to life than this?

At the end of that year, my coach called me out. He didn't accept my excuses. He looked at me and said the thing I didn't want to hear: "You don't play football because you're injured; you don't play because you are scared. Scared of what it might cost you. How hard it might be."

And then he said, "But you don't have to fear hard work."

And then he did the most remarkable thing: He gave me a second chance.

And he, along with the rest of the staff, taught me what to do with it so I wouldn't make the same mistake twice.

What I learned was more than the skills required to play a game. I learned the lessons of toughness, integrity, belief, excellence, effort, and service. The foundation of character and what it means to be part of something bigger than yourself.

My maternal grandparents—who chose to raise me as their own, and whom I called *mom* and *dad* my whole life—believed it takes a village to raise a child. My grandfather worked as a gas man. My grandmother worked in a school cafeteria. They didn't have extra time, money, or energy. But they had an abundance of love. And they believed, without hesitation, that the right environment, the right village could shape a kid that statistics had already written off.

They were right.

■ ■ ■

Going into my senior year of high school, I had done everything I was supposed to do.

Leadership. Grades. Talent. Character. The list was complete. I was an all-state wrestler my junior year, qualified for regionals in discus, and was being recruited to play football at the next level. Every goal I had set was coming true.

But on the first rep of the first scrimmage of my senior season, I tore my ACL.

Just like that, my season was over.

I remember lying in the hospital bed after surgery, talking with my dad. The emotions were real: the doubt, the grief, the weight of everything lost. But underneath all of it, a thought surfaced that I have never forgotten: *Now I get to prove that I am the leader I said I am.*

In a new way.

A way I never had before.

■ ■ ■

At some point, every driven person faces a moment like this. When talent isn't enough and effort isn't the answer. When spiraling circumstances test what you actually believe about adversity. When declining numbers expose whether your optimism was ever real or just conditional. When a hard conversation reveals your relationship with the truth. When selfish ambition quietly starts costing the people around you something they never agreed to pay.

It's in these moments that you have to decide—not just what you are going to do, but who you are going to become.

How you show up in life's hardest moments is not determined by the circumstances. It is determined by the beliefs you have examined, practiced, and held before those moments arrive. That is what this book is about.

Which brings me to the driving question of this book: *Is your character strong enough to carry you through life's hardest moments?*

Not your talent. Not your work ethic. Not your reputation or your results or your résumé.

Your character.

That question deserves an honest answer, and I want to help you find yours. Character isn't something you have. It is something you build. This book will show you exactly where your character is strong enough for the heaviest of life's adversities, and where what you say and what you do are out of alignment.

In Part I: The Framework I'll introduce you to the big idea of this book: Character is the result of your beliefs, practiced over time. Or as I'll define it in Chapter 3:

> *Character is who you are when the pressure is on—the pattern of beliefs and behaviors that consistently guide how you show up in life's hardest moments.*

This definition of character enables character to take a bigger role in governing your life—no longer a static list of traits to possess. In this book character is a daily, dynamic pursuit that is the result of how you choose to live your life when life is most challenging. Shifting our understanding of character from it being a possession to a practice is what enables character to become the competitive advantage that lasts.

In Part II: The Seven Uncommon Beliefs I will introduce you to the seven principles that build a competitive edge that lasts. These seven principles are not just a loose collection of good ideas or teaching stories. They are examined beliefs—born from what I call the *Seven Pressure Tests*, recurring challenges that test you in life and leadership—that have a way of exposing the gap between what you say you believe and what your behavior actually shows.

Those tests are not random.

In 2017 I founded a company called 2Words Character Development (www.2Words.tv). We write, film, and produce a video-based character and leadership development program for students from elementary to varsity sports and host leadership events for high-impact student leaders. Since 2017, we have grown from an idea in my living room to reaching over 2.5 million students, athletes, coaches, and educators across 34 states, including over 60% of the schools in the state of Texas.

Over the last 10 years I have delivered over 1,700 speeches to teams and schools, real estate and insurance companies, collegiate and professional sports teams, hospitals and local governments, and leaders from across disciplines. But no matter where I go, the pressures that I first saw show up in locker rooms are the same ones that show up in boardrooms, hospitals, classrooms, and homes.

Every leader and team I have ever worked with have been tested by the same seven pressures. I call them the *Seven Pressure Tests*:

- Adversity
- Uncertainty
- Identity
- Truth
- Mastery
- Support
- Purpose

■ ■ ■

Before we begin, I want to lay my cards on the table.

The chapters that follow are the most personal thing I've ever written. I believe the best lessons taught are lessons lived, and I've lived every lesson in this book. So while many of the stories are about me, I'm not the hero. The late Brennan Manning captured my heart posture best when he wrote,

> *"I'm just a beggar trying to tell other beggars where to get some bread."*

I've done my best to connect those dots so that wherever you are in your journey—from student athlete to CEO—you can see yourself in these stories.

Every story in this book is real. At times, I will tell the story just as it happened. Other times, I have changed various details to protect a person's identity, and a few times, I have created a composite story from multiple experiences to make the teaching point most clear.

One of the greatest compliments I've ever received came from my friend, mentor, and *New York Times*–best-selling author John U. Bacon. He told me that I wasn't just a good teacher and communicator—I was the kind of leader who other leaders want their kids to listen to. I hope that spirit comes through here and that this book is worth your time at work and worth a conversation with your kids at home.

More than anything, however, my prayer is that this book helps you build the kind of character and competitive edge that lasts.

Let's get to work.

PART

# I

# The Framework

CHAPTER

1

# Never Let Your Talent Outrun Your Character

When was the last time you truly wondered?

Not searched. Not scrolled. Not skimmed for a quick hit of information.

When was the last time you sat with a question long enough for it to press back on you?

The kind of wondering that slows you down. The kind that doesn't immediately reach for an answer but instead pulls you into the tension of not knowing, and forces you to examine things that are uncomfortable and inconvenient.

We have atrophied that muscle. Why bother not knowing an answer when we have access to every answer in the palm of our hand? Why wrestle with a hard question when the answer is a tap away?

Access to information isn't the problem. The habit of not examining the things that need examining is.

Because for the hardest questions life and leadership ask, the answers aren't the point.

Who you become through the examining is.

Information can inform us, but it cannot transform us. It cannot decide for us how we respond under pressure, hold the line when things get hard, or steady our minds when they wander into the deep waters of fear, doubt, or uncertainty. Information cannot govern us.

That's the work of character.

■ ■ ■

I give more than a hundred talks a year, many of them at leadership events hosted by my company, 2Words Character Development. At one of those events, a close friend and athletic director named Charles Ament pushed hard for us to bring in a speaker I had never heard of.

His name was Phil Beckner.

Coach Ament didn't mention it casually. He pressed.

"Mackey," he said, "trust me—Phil's a stud."

Phil works with NBA players, helping them develop the skills that separate good from elite. His résumé included some of the best athletes in the world.

But résumés don't impress me.

A list of accomplishments doesn't tell you much about whether someone can actually teach. I care about one thing:

Can you step in front of a room and make the people there better?

Coach Ament assured me Phil would make every person in the room better, and he was right.

Phil's session was clear, practical, and sharp. He broke things down the way great coaches break down film: simple enough to understand immediately, but layered enough that you could see how it applied in real situations. He shared personal experiences without turning vulnerability into a performance, which is rarer than it should be.

After his talk, I sent him a message with a few observations and some feedback. The way he approached player development felt familiar—like what we try to do with leadership: slow things down enough for people to see what they've been missing.

That message started the relationship and we decided to connect in person.

Phil suggested dinner. His favorite place, he said, was the Cheesecake Factory.

I don't usually have big opinions about chain restaurants, but cheesecake happens to be my favorite dessert, so the decision was simple.

Somewhere between grilled chicken, steamed broccoli, and a slice of caramel cheesecake Phil asked a question that caught me off guard: "If I put you in a room with NBA players," he said, "what would your message be?"

On paper, the answer should have been easy.

I've spent most of my career refining this work: teaching, speaking, challenging young leaders across the country. The message isn't new. I've said it thousands of times.

But at that moment, I hesitated.

I speak primarily to high school athletes. Students. Young leaders who are still becoming who they're going to be. The men Phil works with live in a different world. They're among the most talented, wealthy, and visible athletes on the planet. Kids look up to them. Adults pay to watch them.

And Phil was asking what I would say to them.

For a moment, a quiet thought slipped in, one that didn't need to be loud to be disruptive.

*Who am I to speak to them? I am just "the high school guy."*

Comparison has a way of distorting perspective.

■ ■ ■

I sat with Phil's question for a moment, turning it over in my mind while the noise of the restaurant filled the space around us.

There's always a temptation in moments like that to reach for something impressive—to say something polished or clever, something that sounds like it belongs in a room full of professional athletes.

But he would have seen right through that, and I knew it.

So instead of searching for something impressive, I gave him the answer I believed in the most.

"I'd tell them the same thing I tell my student athletes every day," I said.

Phil leaned in slightly, waiting.

"Never let your talent outrun your character."

I didn't add anything to it. There wasn't anything to add. It wasn't a speech or a framework, just a simple truth I had seen play out too many times to ignore.

Phil nodded almost immediately.

"That's exactly what they need," he said.

I asked him why.

He leaned back in his chair, thinking for a second before answering.

"So many of these guys have been elite their entire lives," he said. "They've been the best players in every gym they've ever walked into. Talent carried them through high school. Talent carried them through college. And when that happens long enough, nobody ever really forces you to build anything underneath it."

That stayed with me.

The players Phil works with already have everything most people spend their lives chasing: talent, opportunity, resources, access. From the outside, it looks like they have every advantage. But even at that level, there is still a kind of limitation that doesn't show up on stat sheets or highlight reels.

It's not your talent. It's your character.

But exceptional talent has a way of creating exemptions. When someone is good enough, doors continue to open even when other parts of their life are still underdeveloped. Success can arrive before the beliefs and behaviors required to sustain it are fully formed.

Over time, that shapes a person's character.

Phil leaned forward again, almost as if he wanted to make sure I understood the weight of what he was saying.

"Our job isn't just to help them win games," he said. "It's to help them win in life. That means helping them develop the kind of edge that lasts after talent evens out."

In life and leadership, your talent is your floor and your character is your ceiling.

Talent opens doors. It creates opportunities. In the early stages, it can feel like the deciding factor—the differences are obvious: One person is faster, sharper, more naturally gifted than everyone else in the room.

But the longer the game goes, the more those differences begin to fade. Other people improve. Experience accumulates. The room gets better. And when that happens, the question changes. It is no longer about who has the most talent; it becomes about who has built the character to sustain what talent started.

That is when people separate.

Not at the beginning—when talent is most visible—but later, when it is no longer enough to carry the weight by itself.

Talent can take you a long way, but it was never meant to carry you the whole way.

■ ■ ■

What that conversation clarified wasn't merely a speech topic for NBA players. It gave language to a clear pattern.

Most of us are introduced to the idea of character early in life. Parents try to anchor it at home. Teachers repeat it in classrooms. Coaches reinforce it in locker rooms. For a time, those lessons were foundational.

But somewhere along the way, something shifts.

As we grow older, character slowly moves from the center of our development to the margins. It remains part of the language we use—printed on posters, referenced in mission statements—but it rarely stays at the center of what we pursue. When decisions are made, when performance is evaluated, when outcomes are measured, and when it's time to solve problems, the focus shifts to talent.

In reality, many of the most persistent leadership challenges are not talent problems at all.

They're character problems.

A team may be talented but lack trust. A leader may have charisma but resist feedback. A high performer may excel when conditions are ideal but unravel when pressure rises.

The issue isn't what they can do. It's who they've become because of what they believe.

*As long as I can keep getting better . . . everything else will take care of itself.*

And for a while, that belief system works.

■ ■ ■

The challenge of this book is this: Instead of asking how far your talent can take you, ask yourself, *Do I have a strong enough character to sustain me as I grow?*

That question changes what you pay attention to. It shifts the focus away from what is most visible and toward what is foundational.

Because over time, talent will level out. The longer you do whatever it is you do in life, the closer you will get to the point where everyone is talented. When the margins of difference narrow—when the pressure increases, when the easy advantages begin to fade—what separates you from others won't just be who has better talent.

It will be who has a stronger character.

Once you see it, it's hard to unsee.

You begin to notice it in the teammate who performs well until something challenges their role. In the leader who is confident until they are questioned. In the organization that looks strong until pressure exposes what hasn't been tested.

And if you're willing, you'll begin to notice it in yourself.

The once quiet moments when your response didn't match your intention or you allowed your standards to slip will get uncomfortably loud. The small gaps between the belief you proclaimed and the character your actions revealed will look wider than the Grand Canyon.

■ ■ ■

Which brings me back to wondering, *I wonder what you will do when you notice?*

Will you jump to your phone and search up the right information or the answer to the question "What do I need to do next?"

Or will you slow down long enough to get brutally honest with yourself about how you are doing on the Seven Pressure Tests life gives you? When the pressures of adversity, uncertainty, identity, truth, mastery, support, and purpose show up in your life—and they will—would you be willing to slow down and examine:

*What do I really believe about this?*

*What belief-driven actions have become patterns in my life?*

*What do my patterns tell me about the truth of my character?*

And maybe most important:

*Is my character strong enough to carry me through life's hardest moments?*

That is the ultimate question that the seven uncommon beliefs of this book will examine. I call them *uncommon beliefs* because they are, to be on the nose about it, so uncommon.

They take the default beliefs of those who put talent first and flip them on their heads. They each demand that you consider a different scoreboard. When these beliefs are examined, and allowed to grow into the patterns that shape the truth of who you are, they work together to produce a competitive advantage that can't be taken from you: your character.

## The Seven Uncommon Beliefs

- **Hard isn't bad.** I am not a victim of adversity. I will get knocked down but I will always get back up—grateful, stronger, and smarter because of it.

- **Optimism requires no evidence.** I choose optimism—not because the outcome is certain, but because certainty was never mine to control. Who I am becoming is more important than what happens.
- **I am not my performance.** I refuse to allow something that can be taken from me to be my foundation. I will daily pursue the examined life.
- **The truth is not my enemy.** I will always receive hard truths, have hard conversations, and pursue the truth—even when it is uncomfortable.
- **Mastery is not the destination.** I refuse to arrive. I will always strive to be better today than I was yesterday—because I am worth that work.
- **I don't have to do it alone.** Independence is not strength. Asking for help is not a sign that something is wrong with me—it's how I show my strength.
- **It's not about me.** I refuse to live or lead in a tit-for-tat system—I don't keep score. I freely give the best of me to whoever is in front of me. Always.

CHAPTER

2

# The Danger of Success

What makes you different?

Not different in theory or potential, but different in substance. What do you bring to the team that actually helps reach the goal? What is it about you—as a leader, a teammate, or a professional—that makes people want to follow you? Why should someone trust you when the stakes are high?

This question is more than a thought exercise. Versions of it appear in real rooms where decisions are made. Sometimes formally, across a desk or a conference table. Sometimes in the whispered conversations that happen after the meeting ends. And sometimes they are never spoken at all, even though everyone in the room is thinking about them.

When someone asks what makes you different, you usually don't need much time to think. The answer arrives quickly—almost automatically. It comes so naturally that you may not even notice the process happening.

That response feels immediate not because you've recently spent hours analyzing it, but because you've been answering some version of that question for most of your life.

Without realizing it, you've been collecting evidence.

Over time, certain moments attach themselves to your understanding of who you are. A coach notices something in you early and gives you more responsibility. A teacher tells you that you solve problems others struggle with. A supervisor trusts you with something difficult, and gives you something harder when you deliver.

Those experiences shape what you believe about what you are capable of and where you belong.

Success reinforces those beliefs. The moments when preparation paid off, when discipline created separation, when your effort helped a group succeed. The painful moments leave their marks as well. The time you trusted someone who let you down. The meeting when you felt unprepared and exposed. The loss that left you determined never to feel that vulnerable again.

What began as a series of experiences becomes something much deeper: a belief about how the world works and how you must operate inside it.

Which is precisely why most people never stop to question it.

■ ■ ■

When I ask leaders and teams what makes them different, the answers are remarkably consistent.

Some talk about what they can do that others cannot. Competency. Talent. Skill. The ability to perform at a level others simply aren't wired or trained to reach.

Others describe what they are willing to do that others will not. The hours. The sacrifice. The discipline required to show up earlier, stay later, and keep working when the applause fades and the room empties.

And others point to what they have done that others have not. Experience. Exposure. Context. They've been in the room longer, learned lessons sooner, made mistakes that translated into insight.

These answers rarely come from ego. They come from lived experience. People live and learn, observe and adjust. Ability creates opportunity. Discipline produces results. Experience sharpens decision-making.

Those lessons sit at the center of what our culture celebrates.

Meritocracy. Hustle. Drive. The belief that your competitive edge comes from doing more, being more, and having what others do not.

The idea is simple: If you can create more separation—more skill, more effort, more experience—you will eventually have your edge.

At first blush this sounds right. It sounds like ambition. It sounds like discipline. It sounds like the kind of internal drive every driven person is supposed to cultivate.

But very quickly that drive becomes a greedy mistress.

No matter how much "more" you give it, it never returns the edge it promised. As soon as you achieve, accomplish, or arrive at the "more" your drive demanded, it drops the news that the terms have changed, and your "more" is no longer enough.

You can protest, but it is useless. If you stop giving what the drive demands, it will find someone else who will, and you will be left behind.

I call it the *bigger bear problem.* It goes like this: There is always a bigger bear in the woods.

No matter how good you are at what you do, there is always someone, somewhere who is smarter, stronger, sharper, bigger, or better than you. There exists, somewhere, someone who wants what you want more than you and is willing to work harder to get it.

So, if you really want this, you must push yourself further, work harder, and sacrifice more than you ever thought possible. No excuses. No shortcuts. Just more work.

Do the work to become the biggest bear in the forest.

The problem, of course, is that if there is always a bigger bear, no matter what you do, it will never be enough.

But that didn't stop me. I figured, *Someone has to be the biggest bear. Why not me?*

I worked constantly and unapologetically. Drove 12 hours round trip for a 20-minute speech. When I felt tired or discouraged, I didn't slow down—I added something else to my plate. Another commitment. Another project. Another challenge to chase.

Rest was not an option—rest was for teddy bears. I was a grizzly.

My alarm was set to a recording of Dr. Eric Thomas's track "I Grind." I let the whole chorus play every morning. It was my mantra.

My wife hated it.

I believed it.

It was my answer to the question, "What makes you different?"

My work ethic, drive, discipline, and relentless effort have always amplified my talent. The successes I had notched in life, the praises I cherished most, and the mistakes I refused to repeat, were all connected to the idea that I could work myself into being the biggest bear in the woods.

When people asked how long I could maintain my pace, I remember feeling genuinely confused by the question. Why would I stop?

This was my competitive edge.

■ ■ ■

It's easy to assume the danger in this mindset appears when it stops working—when the competition catches up, when others match the effort, or when the gap closes—but that is not the danger most leaders actually face. The real danger appears when no one expects.

It does not arrive when your mentality fails.

It appears when it works.

The promotions come. The platform grows. The influence spreads. The calendar fills faster than it ever has before. From the outside, everything looks healthy. From the inside, all the sacrifice feels justified.

But beneath that momentum a subtle shift takes place, one that is almost impossible to see while you are living inside it.

You stop asking why things are working. Not because you no longer care or because you've abandoned your values. But because nothing in your environment requires you to ask anymore.

Success has a way of silencing hard questions.

The boundaries, disciplines, and standards that once kept you grounded don't disappear, but they do begin to feel less rigid. Practices that once shaped restraint start to feel optional. Standards that once guided your decisions start to feel negotiable.

This doesn't happen because you stopped believing in those standards.

It happens because success convinces you that you no longer need to examine your beliefs.

And gradually, you begin asking talent to do more than it was ever designed to do. Talent is meant to produce results—open doors, create opportunities, generate momentum. But when success accelerates, we begin assigning it responsibilities it was never built to carry. We start asking talent to regulate appetite, provide restraint, define meaning, and carry identity.

Talent has never been particularly good at those things.

But when everything around you is still working, that weakness is almost impossible to notice.

Effectiveness begins to masquerade as maturity. Output becomes confused with health. Momentum begins to feel like meaning.

That's the danger of success.

In summer 2024, two things were true: I was at the peak of my professional success, and I had no idea of the gradual but radical shift that had taken place inside of me. I didn't have the words to describe either, but I knew, in my soul, that change was coming.

I remember describing it to a dear friend like this: "We are about to blow up (and get really big) or we are about to blow up (and screw it all up). I'm really not sure which."

■ ■ ■

The biggest coaching event of the year is called *Coaching School*, and is hosted by the Texas High School Coaches Association. Over 17,000 coaches come from across Texas and around the country to learn, network, and grow as coaches. Think of it like this: Coaching School is the monster child of the biggest trade shows, leadership conferences, and professional development seminars you have ever been to.

We take over the host city's convention district. There are coaches at every hotel, restaurant, and Lime bike depot in the city. They are all decked out with lanyards, team polos, and an impressive array of Jordan's. It feels less like a conference and more like an invasion of people who care deeply about the same thing.

When I launched 2Words Character Development in 2017, I had already spent seven years as a volunteer, helping my local high school football team connect the dots between sports and life. I had no idea that that work would become the foundation of a nationwide initiative. I was just a guy who loved his community and believed sports could teach something more than how to win a game. So when I launched the company, I thought maybe 30 schools might sign up.

And the first step in finding those 30 schools was to have a booth at Coaching School.

The first time we attended Coaching School in summer 2017, we were one of hundreds of vendors. Our booth sat in the very back corner of the convention hall, right near the bathrooms. I remember looking at the map and thinking, *Well, everyone has to go sometime.*

But by summer 2024, everything had changed.

Those 30 schools I hoped would use our program had become thousands. We were no longer one of a bunch of vendors. We were one of a handful of the highest level partners. I stood on the same convention floor as 2017 and saw our logo everywhere.

We had become the official character and leadership development program of the Texas High School Coaches Association. More than half the schools in Texas were using one of our programs. Schools in over 30 states had adopted the curriculum.

Over those seven school years, I had driven hundreds of thousands of miles, delivered 1,700 speeches, and affected millions of students and coaches.

By every measurable standard, I was successful.

And yet, as I walked the floor that year—shaking hands, smiling for pictures, answering the same questions I'd answered hundreds of times before—I felt something I could not explain.

It wasn't pride. It wasn't gratitude. It was an overwhelming sense of dread. A tightness in my chest that never quite released. The lurking sense that something was about to collapse.

■ ■ ■

There was no single crisis. No headline-worthy failure. Just the quiet accumulation of weeks that never slowed down, expectations that never lifted, and a calendar that refused to leave room for anything except more.

About three weeks after Coaching School, I was on my way to a weeklong stretch of speaking events when my wife told me she didn't care if I came home.

Even now, those words are difficult to say out loud.

Sadly, my first reaction wasn't panic or grief or even a sudden reality check.

It was a calculation.

*This will pass. I just need to get through one more week. The money is worth the sacrifice. Then we'll figure it out. We've been through this before. This is just a season.*

Momentum always whispers the same lie: that the next finish line will finally give you room to breathe.

On the way to the airport, my best friend and right-hand person at 2Words, Colton, called.

He didn't call to communicate important logistics about the week of travel, motivate me as I went to push the business forward, or wish me safe travels. He called to confront me.

"What the hell are you doing, man?"

Instead of hearing his concern for my family and my life outside of work, I felt irritated. Instead of pausing to consider what he was saying, I started calculating the cost of changing plans—canceling the event, refunding the money, disappointing the organizers, and damaging my reputation—and lobbying for why neither of us or the company could afford for me to go home and "deal with family stuff."

It is embarrassing to admit now, but at that moment I was more worried about the hit my reputation would take for canceling a speaking engagement than I was about the implications of the words my wife had spoken.

That realization still unsettles me.

That's how far I had drifted.

I remember exactly where I was standing when I decided to cancel the trip and go home. Ten more steps and I would have been through security. Twenty more minutes and I would have boarded the flight.

Here is the uncomfortable part: If I had boarded that plane, those speeches would have gone incredibly well. I would have crushed it.

The audience would have applauded. The feedback would have been glowing. People would have lined up to tell me how much the message meant to them. By every external measure, it would have looked like another successful week.

My talent would have carried me forward into even more opportunities.

And no one in that room would have known that while I was helping them build their lives, my own was quietly falling apart.

■ ■ ■

I didn't feel successful. I felt untethered.

So I turned around, walked back to the parking garage, and drove home.

Somewhere on North Hwy 281, the truth of my reality landed me with the weight of a thousand elephants.

I wasn't Superman.

I was a man who cared more about his work than his family.

That was the moment everything inverted.

What had once been an expression of character had slowly become a substitute for it. The discipline that once protected my priorities was now demanding more than it should. The drive that once reflected conviction was now leading me 100 mph down a dead end street.

Failure had never threatened me the way success did.

Too often, people wait for something to go wrong before they stop and look at what's underneath. But success is a helluva drug. It keeps asking for—no, taking a little more—one more commitment, one more yes, one more week, until one day you look up and realize there's nothing left to give.

The image that comes to mind is *The Lorax*.

Cut down one more tree. Then another. Then another. Not because you're malicious, but because the machine you've built only knows how to do one thing: keep going.

Keep biggering. And BIGGERING. AND BIGGERING.

Until one day, there are no trees left.

CHAPTER

# 3

# Character as Governance

Think about the last time you pushed past reasonable. Past tired. Past the point where a sensible person would have stopped.

What drove you forward?

Had you asked me in those weeks leading up to Coaching School I would have told you I was driven by a deep sense of responsibility to my family, my team, and the mission of my work—and I would have genuinely meant it. What I wouldn't have told you, and to this day I don't know if I even had words for it, was that that responsibility had begun to feel like a burden, like the sacrifices I was making were the price I had to pay to make the impact I wanted to make.

The responsibility-to-burden shift should have been a sign. It wasn't.

I should have seen that my unhealthy drive for more had very little to do with my family. I didn't.

Had I been examining my life, I would have seen that my goals had become unhealthy, because healthy goals never require an unhealthy sacrifice.

But I missed all of that. Why? Because I was living an unexamined life, driven by one part fear and one part reward.

*Fear* sounds like responsibility at first. It says, "I can't afford to fail. I don't want to let people down. I don't want to go back to where I came from."

For a season, fear protects you—it keeps you sharp, keeps you prepared, keeps you from being careless. But fear never asks, "Who are you becoming?" It only asks, "What are you avoiding?" Over time, it demands more certainty, more control, more of you. It slowly manipulates you to believe that rest is risky, delegation is dangerous, and trusting others is a liability you can't afford.

*Reward* feels more intuitive. It says, "If I do this, I'll get that."

*Just a little more work for one more win. Just a little more sacrifice for a little more recognition.*

Reward works because it's a positive feedback loop—the effort pays off, people notice, results show up. But the more rewards you get, the more reward becomes a prerequisite for you to work. Praise has to be both loud and unique before you do the work. Wins have to get bigger and more noticeable to spur you to action.

Fear and reward aren't shallow motivations. They're immature ones—necessary early, but dangerous if never outgrown. Why are they dangerous? Because they work.

With enough talent, you can outrun the consequence you fear and chase down the reward you want . . . for a while, anyways.

This is where smart, disciplined people begin to rationalize: *This is temporary. This is just the season. This is the cost of leadership*.

And that's exactly why it's so hard to notice when it starts driving you.

But make no mistake: In summer 2024 fear and reward were driving me.

So how did I get there?

Yes, my pace was nonstop, but I didn't lose my values; I didn't stop believing the right things; I didn't wake up one day and decide character didn't matter.

I asked my talent to do more than it was ever meant to do. I stopped examining my life.

What I lost was not character as virtue but character as governance.

Character, at its core, isn't just about knowing what's right. It's about what regulates you when talent accelerates or when things go wrong. It's the internal operating system that determines how much is enough, when to stop, what you refuse to trade, and who you are becoming in the process. It's what should have told me that my family mattered more than my speaking calendar. It didn't—because I stopped examining my beliefs and allowed my talent to determine how I showed up.

Long before we had terms like character development or leadership formation, Aristotle described how character is formed. He called the process habituation.[1] His insight was simple: We do not become courageous by admiring courage, but by practicing courageous action until it becomes part of our nature.

Character, what Aristotle understood as virtue, is not a gift received. It is not a personality trait you're born with or a quality you either have or don't. It is something you build through repeated action, deliberate practice, and the slow accumulation of choices that shape who you become.

Character is not built in the moment of pressure.

It is revealed there.

Character is not a trait but a pattern.

It's not something you possess, but something you practice. The beliefs you hold and the choices you make are always shaping your character—whether you intend that or not.

That's why I define character this way: *Character is who you are when the pressure is on—the pattern of beliefs and behaviors that consistently guide how you show up in life's hardest moments.*

Talent produces outcomes. Character governs direction.

Talent answers the question, *What can I do?*

Character asks the harder question, *Why am I doing this?*

And one harder still, *Who am I becoming in the process?*

## The Cycle

If I could simplify the character development process down to a model, I would call it *the Cycle* and it would look like this:

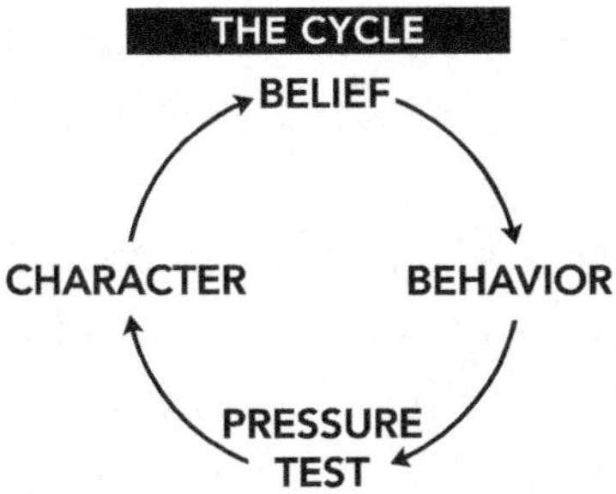


What you believe determines your behavior.

Your behaviors are pressure tested.

The pressure tests reveal the truth about your character—not who you intended or aspired to be, but the results of the choices you repeatedly made when no one was keeping score.

There are no shortcuts in this system and you can't cheat it. The Cycle is always running. The only question is whether you're paying attention to what it's showing you.

In 2024, the Cycle revealed a truth about myself I was unwilling to live with: I cared more about work than my family.

The Cycle offered me an examination and a truth that my talent could never give me.

An examination of what was driving me, what I believed, the behaviors I practiced, and the truth about the man I had become. It showed me what I call *Integrity Gaps*.

## Integrity Gaps

You've probably seen the commercials.

You've been taunted by Ving Rhames. You've been conditioned so thoroughly that at the mere mention of the word

*Arby's*, synapses trained by years of repetition fire before you've even decided to—completing the sentence: "ARBY'S . . . We have the meats."

Since 2014, Arby's has run some of the most persuasive food advertising in the business. The brisket glistening under studio lighting. The steak nuggets described with the kind of specificity that makes you wonder if maybe, just maybe, Arby's really is your new favorite steakhouse.

Intellectually, you know better. You've been here before. The roast beef in the picture is never the roast beef on the tray.

But then you hear the description of the steak nuggets, and something in you wonders.

So you get in the truck and drive down to Arby's.

Only to find out that they most definitely do not have the "meats."

The product and the commercial were miles apart. Expectation and reality were two completely different things. The marketing and the meal had a gap between them that no amount of Arby's sauce could close.

Now—before you get too high and mighty about your fast food opinions—consider that most of us are running the same campaign.

Not with roast beef. With our beliefs.

We say we believe accountability matters. We say we value growth. We say we're committed to honesty, to excellence, to showing up for the people who are counting on us. We put it in the handbook. We say it in the staff meeting. We post it on the wall.

And then Monday arrives.

And the gap between what we say we believe and what the Cycle reveals to be true is visible.

This is the Integrity Gap.

When the Cycle reveals an Integrity Gap, it is not a judgment of what you did or didn't do. It is simply a diagnosis. What you do with that diagnosis will tell you more about your character than almost anything else.

Sometimes, the best way to demonstrate your character is to admit that you have an Integrity Gap in the first place.

While this examination is deeply personal, it doesn't need to happen in isolation.

I spent many hours having hard, tearful conversations with my wife. We did the work. I reconnected to the people in my life: the relationships with my team, and the coaches and students we serve—not the mission, not the numbers, not the logo on the convention banners: the people. I committed to working in a way that served my family instead of in a way that just cost them.

In short, when I was shown my Integrity Gap, I did the work to change my beliefs, and my behaviors followed.

I rewrote my travel schedule. Eliminated everything that could be eliminated—including all social media. I put boundaries on when, where, and how I would show up. Not because I stopped caring about the work, but because I finally understood that the work without the governance of my character would keep taking until there was nothing left to give.

When the pressure test came, what was revealed was altogether different. Before this examination, there was dread. A low-hum of fear underneath everything: *Don't. Mess. This. Up.*

Every opportunity felt like a test I might fail. Every success carried the anxiety of losing it.

That's the ultimate problem with building your competitive edge on something that can be taken away: It's only a matter of time before it is.

But when your competitive edge *is character*—something that can never be taken from you (only given away)—confidence and passion replace the anxiety of "never making a mistake." Fear and reward are replaced by a healthy drive fueled by service, growth, and "want to." Not because you have to. Not because the scoreboard demands it. Because the work itself is worth doing, and the people it serves are worth showing up for.

■ ■ ■

So I wonder, What is the Cycle saying is true about you right now?

Not what you want to be true. Not what used to be true. What is true right now about your beliefs, your behaviors, your patterns, and your response to pressure?

What Integrity Gaps do you have?

Does fear and reward run your beliefs and behaviors the way a point guard runs an offense? Has your talent been so all-consuming that you haven't had time or reason to stop and consider what is governing you?

Or are you driven by service, growth, and want to? Have you found the healthy boundaries that make your talent work for you, instead of you working for your talent?

The Cycle isn't a ladder you climb once and then stand on. It is a living process. It runs in every area of your life simultaneously: Some areas hold, some areas are fragile, some areas not yet examined at all.

The Cycle is the work you must do, and the uncomfortable truth you must confront.

## Note

1. Aristotle, *Nicomachean Ethics*, Book II. Standard Ebooks, n.d.

# CHAPTER 4

# The Seven Pressure Tests

In sports, coaches say, "The film doesn't lie."

You can question a coach's decision or argue with the referee's decision, but put it on film and the truth is right there, frame by frame, unedited and unsparing.

In business, you would say the bottom line is black and white. Revenue either came in or it didn't. The numbers don't have feelings.

The Cycle works the same way. It doesn't give partial credit or grade on a curve. It has no bias. It simply reveals—with complete accuracy—what is true about what you actually believe.

But it doesn't reveal everything, everywhere all at once.

There are specific moments—recurring places where pressure has a way of finding the Integrity Gap between what you say you believe and what your character actually shows. Those places are not random. In every leader I have ever worked with, in every team I have ever sat with, in my own life on the days that are embarrassing to remember—the gap shows up in the same seven places.

I call them the *Seven Pressure Tests.*

A pressure test isn't a diagnosis. The Cycle is the diagnosis. A pressure test is the kind of weight that, when applied, gives the Cycle something to reveal. Adversity is one. Uncertainty is another. There are five more. Each of them is a recurring load that every person eventually has to carry, and each of them—when the weight comes—exposes whether the belief underneath your behavior was strong enough to hold.

You don't get to choose whether you encounter them. All seven are coming for you.

What you do get to choose is whether you look honestly at what they reveal.

That is the work the rest of this book is built on.

## The Seven Pressure Tests

Each of the Seven Pressure Tests is paired with one uncommon belief—an examined conviction strong enough to govern behavior when the pressure arrives. Each chapter that follows is built on one of those seven uncommon beliefs: where it comes from, what it looks like when it's missing, and what changes when it takes root.

And each of those chapters ends in the same place: with a pressure test.

The pressure test is not another diagnostic. The Cycle has already done the diagnostic work. The pressure test is your turn—the moment at the end of each chapter when you stop reading about the belief and look honestly at what the Cycle has revealed. Not in theory. Not last year. Right now, in the pressure test that chapter just walked you through.

That is by design. Every chapter ends with you: Are you in alignment with your beliefs or is there an Integrity Gap that needs closing?

Remember: Integrity exists in closing the gap—not in never needing to. Looking, honestly, at the pressure test is where the closing begins.

What follows is the first pass at all Seven Pressure Tests. The goal is not to solve anything. The goal is just to notice what flinches when you read it.

That flinch is information.

That is where the work begins.

## Adversity

Adversity is an equal opportunity employer. It comes for all of us. You are either in a hard season, coming out of a hard season, or headed toward one. There is nowhere else to be.

Which means the question is never whether adversity will arrive.

The question is what you believe it means when it does.

Think about the last hard thing that landed in your week. Did you treat it as something happening *to* you—proof of unfair conditions, bad timing, someone else's failure—or as something happening *for* you, the kind of weight that, carried honestly, builds something?

Most people tell themselves they handle adversity well. The Cycle tells the truth.

Coach Allen Wilson, the legendary East Texas football coach of the Tyler John Tyler Lions, said it plainly: "You have no philosophy if you haven't lived your philosophy out in the fire." Your beliefs don't reveal themselves in comfortable conditions. They reveal themselves under pressure. And the belief that gets revealed most quickly is what you actually think *hard* means.

Hard days aren't fun for anyone. But they can be fuel for everyone. You decide which.

***When something doesn't go your way, what's the first story you tell yourself about why?***

## Uncertainty

You can't control tomorrow. You can prepare for it, work toward it, make decisions today that improve your odds. But the outcome was never yours to guarantee.

Most of us spend years trying to crack the formula. Work hard enough, prepare thoroughly enough, make the right moves—and the result will follow. And for a while it works.

Which is why uncertainty feels like such a threat. If the right formula is the goal, a broken formula means I have missed the goal.

Spoiler alert: The formula always breaks.

Uncertainty isn't testing whether you can predict outcomes. It is testing whether you have made peace with the fact that you can't—and whether who you are in the not knowing is strong enough to keep moving anyway.

When the path forward is unclear, watch yourself. Do you start cataloguing reasons it won't work? Do you reach for the can't before you've decided who you're going to be? Or do you start from a different premise: *I don't know if there's a way, but I know who I'm going to be while I look for one.*

One is fear running the formula. The other is the predecision running the work.

***When the outcome is unclear, what does your behavior reveal about what you actually believe?***

## Identity

Finish this sentence: *I did 99 things right . . .*

Most people can finish it without help. *And I did one thing wrong*. And that one thing is the only thing they remember.

The 99 disappears as if it never happened. The one is all you can see.

That is what an identity tied to performance does. It doesn't track results—it uses them. Every win becomes evidence you are valuable. Every failure becomes evidence you are not. Your worth rises and falls with the scoreboard, which means your sense of self is only ever as stable as your last outcome.

The cost isn't dramatic. It's a slow erosion in which the moments that should have grounded you—the wins that should have given you confidence, the failures that should have taught you something—become evidence in a case you keep prosecuting against yourself.

The leaders who separate aren't the ones who never fail. They are the ones whose worth is grounded somewhere the scoreboard can't reach.

***When your last significant failure happened, how long did it take before you felt like yourself again—and what does that tell you?***

## Truth

The truth doesn't pick sides. It doesn't strategize for an outcome or demand a response. It is a fixed reality that gives you the freedom to fight it or accept it.

And most people fight it.

Think about the last piece of feedback that stung. Real feedback, not the kind that's easy to receive because it confirms what you already wanted to believe. The kind that landed somewhere it wasn't welcome.

What did you do with it?

Did you push back, diminish, defend? Did you spend the next three days building a case for why it was wrong: gathering evidence, replaying conversations, finding witnesses? Or did you write it down and ask *what else?*

The truth was the same in both responses. The response was different.

Over time, the people who treat truth as an ally outgrow the people who treat it as a threat. Not because they are smarter. Because the truth has been allowed to do its work in them.

***Who in your life is allowed to tell you something you don't want to hear, and when did you last make it easy for them to do it?***

## Mastery

Most people don't quit at the bottom. They quit at the level that finally feels comfortable.

The bottom is a hard place to stay. You can feel the gap between where you are and where you are not, and it pulls effort out of you whether you want it to or not. The work is obvious. The reason to keep working is obvious.

What is dangerous is the level just past that: the level where things are finally working.

When the goals you're pursuing stop requiring your best, watch what happens to your discipline. Fewer reps. Fewer hard conversations. Fewer questions you don't already know the answer to. The work that got you here slowly stops being the work you are doing. The skills you built are now skills you use, not skills you sharpen.

You don't decide to settle. You drift into it. And the drift always feels earned.

Mastery is not a level you arrive at. It is a way-of-being that drives you forward, beyond what you thought you were capable of.

***When in your life have you mistaken a plateau for a finish line?***

## Support

Look at what you are carrying right now.

The thing nobody around you fully knows about. The weight you've decided is yours alone—the project that's getting harder, the relationship that's getting heavier, the season that's getting lonelier the longer it goes on.

Why haven't you asked for help with it?

The answer is almost always some version of the same belief. *Asking for help would expose weakness. Relying on others would mean losing control. Carrying it alone is my responsibility*.

That belief has a ceiling. And driven people hit it every time.

The people around you can see what you're carrying. They have been waiting for an invitation that never comes—not because they don't want to help, but because you have made it clear, without saying a word, that needing them isn't something you do.

Real strength doesn't show up in never needing help. It shows up in the willingness to ask for it.

You are only as strong as you are willing to ask for help.

***What are you carrying alone right now that you haven't asked for help with, and what do you tell yourself is the reason?***

## Purpose

Think about the last time you went out of your way for someone on your team.

Now answer honestly: Somewhere underneath the act—even faintly, even in a corner of your mind you'd rather not look at—were you expecting something back?

Maybe not a favor. Maybe just loyalty. Maybe just the satisfaction of knowing it would come around eventually. Maybe just the self-satisfaction that you are the kind of leader who pours into people.

That tally is a form of tit-for-tat accounting. And most leaders do it.

The good ones don't run selfish math. They run generous math. *Pour into your people and they'll run through walls for you. Serve your team and they'll follow you anywhere.* The inputs are humane. The outputs are real. The math actually works.

But it is still math.

The leaders who separate aren't the ones running better math. They are the ones who threw the ledger out the window, who serve without consulting the math, because the math was never the point.

These leaders put others first. They serve without expectation. Give without demanding repayment. They play a whole different game.

***When you serve the people you lead, what are you quietly expecting back?***

## The Map

Each one of these Seven Pressure Tests reaches past your talent and asks a harder question: What do you actually believe?

The leaders who thrive aren't the ones with more talent or better systems. They are the ones whose beliefs have been examined deeply enough to govern their behavior in the hardest moments life and leadership have to offer.

What follows is not a book about leading others.

It is a book about leading yourself first—the work that has to happen before you have any business leading anyone else. The work most leaders skip. The work you'll wish you had done when the pressure is on and everyone is counting on you.

In Part II, each chapter is built on one of the seven uncommon beliefs that will help you build a competitive edge that lasts. One chapter, one belief, one pressure test.

| The Pressure Test | The Belief |
|---|---|
| Adversity | Hard Isn't Bad |
| Uncertainty | Optimism Requires No Evidence |
| Identity | I Am Not My Performance |
| Truth | The Truth Is Not My Enemy |
| Mastery | Mastery Is Not the Destination |
| Support | I Don't Have to Do It Alone |
| Purpose | It's Not About Me |

The book offers no formulas and no shortcuts. Only a mirror to see yourself clearly with and a refusal to let you off the hook.

You will not get a chapter that resolves cleanly. You will not get cheap inspiration or a feel-good story. You will get an uncommon belief, examined carefully enough to hold, and then the opportunity placed in front of you to examine your own life and beliefs.

■ ■ ■

The single most haunting line I have ever heard a speaker deliver came from author Ian Morgan Cron.

> *"This is life. These are its terms. What are you going to do about it?"*

When we are confronted with reality—the way these Seven Pressure Tests confront us, the way the Cycle confronts us—we are not given the luxury of negotiation. This is life. The terms of our present reality are set.

The only say we get is in what we are going to do about it.

That is why I am convinced that the work of character development is so important. It is our character that enables us to answer Cron's question in a way that produces hope. Hope that what is here today doesn't have to be here tomorrow. The person I see in the mirror doesn't have to always be the same. That I am not limited by my talent, but by my willingness to examine my beliefs, behaviors, and ultimately, my character.

The beliefs that follow aren't uncommon because they are secret.

They will prove uncommon because they are really hard to live out, and very few people are willing to do the work to make them true in their own life.

In the pages to come we are going to examine these uncommon beliefs together, look in the mirror together, and decide what we are going to do about it.

Let's get to work.

PART

# II

# The Seven Uncommon Beliefs

CHAPTER

# 5

# Hard Isn't Bad

> I am not a victim of adversity. I will get knocked down but I will always get back up—grateful, stronger, and smarter because of it.

Twenty minutes before my best lift of the competition, Arnold Schwarzenegger walked through the backstage area.

I don't know how else to describe it except to say that reality split.

The crowd parted. People shouted his name. Phones materialized from thin air—arms extended, voices cracking, grown men and women suddenly transformed into starstruck teenagers. He moved through the space like a force of nature, stopping here, nodding there, absorbing the weight of what he meant to every person in that room.

And he meant something to all of us. Every single person in that building had been shaped by him in some way—through his life, a film, book, or even a phrase.

I just stood there.

I didn't reach for my phone. I didn't try to get his attention or position myself for a photo. I just watched—fully present, trying to hold the moment in my mind rather than reduce it to an image I'd scroll past later.

The room was electric in a way you didn't just hear. You felt it. In your chest. Under your skin.

This was the Arnold Classic—one of the most prestigious strength competitions in the world. I was there to compete in the Armlifting USA grip strength championship.

More than a thousand people were gathered at the main stage to watch us compete, and tens of thousands more roamed the convention hall. My best friend was in the front row. My family was watching from home online. And I was backstage, minutes away from competing in the biggest competition of my adult life, in a sport I competed in, just for me.

That last part mattered more than I expected it to.

I work hard to give everything I can to other people. Speaking, coaching, leading, building—it is all outward. All for someone else. But this—the training, the competition, the long hours in the gym before anyone else was awake—this was mine. Just for me. The most personal and, in the best sense of the word, selfish thing I had done in a long time.

Pride. Anticipation. Sweaty palms. A roller coaster in my stomach that felt less like nerves and more like being fully alive.

Twenty minutes later, everything changed.

■ ■ ■

Armlifting is set up similar to a powerlifting event. There are three events, each testing a different facet of grip strength. The more you lift, the higher your score.

For more than a year I had trained for this moment. My schedule had revolved around it. Twice a week, every week, I worked on specific implements. I adjusted my training, managed my recovery, and made decisions about my time and energy based on what would best prepare me for this stage. The Rogue Axle Double Overhand Deadlift was my best event, and it was the first event of the competition.

As the weights increased throughout the event, I felt more confident, not less. The bar was moving well. My grip felt strong. I made what I believed was a smart decision to skip from 418 pounds to 440 pounds, a weight I had already lifted in competition, thinking it would enable me to conserve enough grip strength to take a bigger lift later.

When I stepped up to the bar at 440 pounds, nothing felt rushed. I set my feet, reached down, and wrapped my hands around the axle. The thickness of the 2-inch bar forced me to squeeze harder than a standard barbell would, but that was familiar. I tightened everything and began the pull.

The weight came off the ground cleanly. It passed my knees. Everything about the lift felt exactly the way it was supposed to feel. I had been in this position before—many times—and I knew what was coming next.

Or at least I thought I did.

The bar stalled just short of lockout. Close enough that I could feel the finish, but not close enough to complete it. For a brief moment, I held it there, trying to will it the rest of the way, but there was nothing left to give.

The bar dropped.

It is a strange thing how quickly a moment can shift. Just seconds earlier, everything had felt aligned. I was executing a plan built over months of preparation. Then, almost instantly, my world flipped upside down.

As I stepped off the platform, the physical part of the lift was over—but the mental lift had just begun. My mind went back to the lift and began replaying it again and again. I could feel the point where the lift slowed, the impact of my decision to skip a weight, and the technical breakdown that had cost me the lockout.

The questions followed almost immediately.

*Had I just compromised the whole competition? Was that decision a mistake? Had I miscalculated something I should have seen coming?*

From there, the questions became less about the lift and more about me.

*Was I strong enough to be here? Did I belong on this stage? Had I invested an entire year of training on an assumption that wasn't actually true?*

There is a noticeable shift that happens in moments like that. The questions stop being exploratory and start becoming declarative. They move from uncertainty to judgment.

*You're not good enough. You don't belong here. You just embarrassed yourself.*

By the time I made it backstage, the physical adrenaline of the lift had been replaced by something heavier. My stomach was tight. My thoughts were scattered. I felt frustrated, disoriented, and uncertain, which is a difficult place to be.

What made the moment more complicated was the fact that I had spent years teaching others how to respond to situations exactly like this one. I have stood in front of large groups of student athletes and explained how to process a mistake, how to move on, how to compete with clarity after something goes wrong.

But standing there backstage, I realized something uncomfortable.

I was not sure I believed what I had been teaching.

I did not feel composed. I did not feel confident. I did not feel ready to step back into competition and execute. The ideas I had communicated so clearly to others felt distant and difficult to access.

That was the Integrity Gap—not as a concept I had taught, but as something I was standing inside.

The real question was not whether I could recover physically.

It was whether I actually believed what I said I believed.

Life had just administered me a pressure test.

## Every Day Is an Interview

Standing backstage, it became clear that what I was experiencing had very little to do with the bar.

The lift was over. The result wasn't changing. But something else was unfolding in real time, and it felt more significant than the miss.

It felt like I was being evaluated.

Not by a judge with a clipboard or a scoreboard tracking results, but by the moment itself. The questions I was asking myself, the conclusions I was starting to draw, the way my posture and attention were changing—it all felt like a response to something pressing in on me.

That is when an idea came back to me—something I had heard but had never felt this directly until that moment.

Every day is an interview.

We think of interviews as scheduled moments where something is on the line—where we prepare, present ourselves, and shape the narrative. We understand that interviews matter because they determine our access to opportunities.

But the most important interviews are not scheduled.

They do not come with a clear beginning or end. They show up in moments—often inconvenient ones—when something does not go the way we expected. When effort does not produce the outcome we believed it would.

In those moments, something is being revealed.

Not our résumé. Not our intentions.

What is being revealed is the truth of what we believe.

Standing backstage, I could see that clearly. The situation itself had not told me I was not good enough. Those conclusions were coming from somewhere else—from the way I was interpreting what had happened.

That interpretation was rooted in belief.

Adversity strips away rehearsed responses and carefully constructed images and reveals what is underneath. The response that comes out in those moments is not manufactured. It is not polished. It is not strategic.

It is honest.

I was not just dealing with a missed lift.

I was in the middle of an interview.

The question being asked was not about strength or technique. The question was, "What do you believe when things don't go your way?"

■ ■ ■

Here is what actually happened in the seconds after the bar dropped.

The weight hadn't changed. The preparation hadn't disappeared. My best friend was still in the front row. My family was still watching. The crowd that had felt electric 20 minutes earlier was still there.

Nothing external had shifted.

But inside, the story had already rewritten itself.

A single missed attempt became evidence of something larger. The gap between what I expected and what happened filled—instantly, automatically—with meaning I hadn't consciously chosen.

*Something is wrong. You don't belong here. This was a mistake.*

That is not a unique response to a missed opportunity. It is the default response most people carry into adversity—the unexamined, common belief that hard means wrong.

Not just difficult. Wrong.

As if difficulty itself is proof that something is off track, unfair, or not meant to be.

It rarely shows up as a stated conviction. It lives in the questions we ask when things don't go our way.

*Why is this happening to me? Why is this so hard? Why does it seem easier for everyone else? What is wrong with me?*

Those questions are honest to our experience. Reasonable, even. But underneath them is an assumption that almost never gets examined—that things should not be this hard in the first place.

Consider this: When you make a mistake, how quick are you to make an excuse or find an explanation outside yourself? If you can save face by blaming a bad break, a teammate, or external conditions, do you? In my experience—and I am willing to bet yours, too—the discomfort of a failure or mistake is something you try to reduce as quickly as possible.

What do you do when a challenge stretches your current ability and the mistakes native to growth start piling up? Do you interpret those as a sign that success is unlikely and pull back to hinge you know you are good at? I won't ask you to answer out loud.

When *hard* is believed to be bad, it becomes a signal to step back, get away, or change course.

And the longer that belief operates unchallenged, the more it becomes self-fulfilling. *Hard* feels overwhelming because we have never developed the capacity to stay inside it.

The only way to develop the capacity to do hard things is to do hard things—especially moments we are most tempted to avoid.

Backstage at the Arnold Classic, there was nowhere to hide. I was standing in the middle of an Integrity Gap I didn't know I had.

Until I did.

## The Uncommon Belief

**Hard isn't bad.** I am not a victim of adversity. I will get knocked down but I will always get back up—grateful, stronger, and smarter because of it.

---

Read that again.

Not as a motivational phrase, but as a claim about how the world actually works—and who you can choose to be inside of it.

The uncommon belief "Hard isn't bad" does three things that the common belief cannot.

First, it rejects the victim's posture. Not as a denial of reality—adversity is real, circumstances are real, outcomes are real. There are things that happen outside your control, and pretending otherwise doesn't make you stronger. But being honest about reality does not require surrendering responsibility for how you respond to it. Adversity creates the situation. It does not control the meaning. And if it does not control the meaning, it does not control what happens next.

Second, this uncommon belief reframes the demand. Hard isn't bad unless you choose to make it bad. Difficulty, by itself, does not carry a fixed meaning—it creates a demand. A demand for more attention, effort, clarity, or belief. If that demand is interpreted as a problem, the focus shifts toward escape. But if it is interpreted as an opportunity, something changes. Hard becomes a chance to see what is actually there—if your preparation was sufficient for task, where Integrity Gaps exist, what the difference is between what you say you value and what you actually do when following through becomes costly.

The question shifts from *Why is this happening to me?* to *What is this asking of me?*

That shift does not remove adversity, but it does change how you engage with it.

Finally, this uncommon belief commits your effort to the response. Getting knocked down is not the defining part of this belief. Getting back up is. And that response is not automatic—gratitude does not naturally follow disappointment, strength does not automatically come from difficulty, growth is not guaranteed by experience alone. Those outcomes require engagement. A willingness to look at the moment honestly, take responsibility where it is required, and continue moving forward even when stepping back would be easier.

Grateful. Stronger. Smarter.

Not because the adversity was pleasant.

Because we believed the adversity wasn't bad.

Stanford psychologist Alia Crum's research on stress mindset found that people who believe stress is harmful perform worse—while people who believe stress is enhancing perform better, show greater focus, and recover more effectively. The adversity itself wasn't the determining factor.

The belief about adversity was.

## Adversity's Big Question

Adversity doesn't RSVP to your life. It shows up unannounced and unwelcomed, at the most inconvenient times.

Sometimes adversity comes from outside your control—a decision made by someone else, conditions that don't match what you prepared for, a call that doesn't go your way. The natural reaction is to focus on what can't be changed. But when the uncommon belief holds, the question shifts from why the situation exists to what can be done within it. What is still available? What is still yours to control?

Other times adversity comes through people—a teammate's mistake, a leader's decision you disagree with, someone else's choice that creates a situation you now have to respond to. While you cannot control their choices, you are still responsible for your own. The question becomes less about what they should have done and more about what you are going to do now that they have done it.

Adversity can also come from your own decisions: When you play stupid games, you win stupid prizes.

For all of us, there is at least one choice you would change in hindsight, a lapse in preparation that becomes visible at the worst possible time. These moments carry a different weight because of the clarity they bring. They show, without much room for interpretation, where something needs to change. And if that is accepted rather than avoided, they become some of the most valuable lessons you will ever learn.

However adversity arrives in your life, it always asks one big question: "What do you believe and is your character strong enough to govern what you do next?"

■ ■ ■

Knowing the "right" belief isn't enough.

You can intellectually understand everything in this chapter and still find yourself backstage at your own Arnold Classic—stomach tight, thoughts scattered, watching the gap between what you believe and what you do widen in real time.

What bridges that Integrity Gap is not more information.

It is a process.

I call it the *Get Right Process*. It's a checklist: five areas that together provide a clear picture of how you are showing up in a difficult moment and five specific practices that help you "get right" when the moment has gone wrong.

I used it backstage that day at the Arnold. And you can, too, when adversity shows up unannounced.

## The Get Right Process

**1. Get Your ALIGNMENT Right:** What kind of person do you want to be?

Backstage, the question that cut through everything else was this: *How would I want my kids to respond in this moment? Am I being the example or the exception?*

That question did something the self-critical voice couldn't. It moved me from self-protection to identity. The value of the experience—and of myself—wasn't found in the result. I was there because I had done the work to earn the right to be there. That was still true whether the bar moved or not.

Your actions in the face of adversity are unmistakable evidence of who you are. Do your character, wants, and work align—or is there an Integrity Gap? The Cycle is at its best in the face of adversity. Don't look away from what it reveals.

**Get Right Practice:** In the face of adversity, return to a positive affirmation that is both earned and true. It should include (1) a declaration of who you are choosing to be in this moment, (2) the work or preparation you have done to have earned your place in the moment, and (3) a refusal to let circumstances take away what is yours to hold.

---

**2. Get Your MIND Right:** Are you willing to let go of your expectations to deal with your reality?

The expectation I had to release was the one that said the first event should have gone well. It didn't. That was the reality.

Fighting it kept me anchored to something I could no longer change. The moment I was willing to let the expectation go, and deal in reality, the rest of the competition came back into focus.

Too often we get so caught up in what we expected that we miss what's happening in reality. Mental toughness is as much about adjusting to an unelected reality as it is about enduring a challenging one.

**Get Right Practice:** When adversity strikes, pause to visualize the next right step. Engage your senses: What will you see, feel, hear, smell, and taste when you take the next smallest step? See yourself executing the next moment well, not relitigating the last one. Then take action.

---

**3. Get Your BODY Right:** How do you want to show up?

When it was time for me to Get Right, I made physical shifts: I untucked my shirt and changed my shoes. Admittedly, they were small actions—almost trivial—but they were deliberate. I was signaling to myself that the previous lift was over and something new was beginning. The body leads the mind more than we realize.

Moving past failure is as much a physical shift as it is an internal one. Your body language is always communicating. What is it saying about you?

**Get Right Practice:** A physical reset routine—something that interrupts the stress response and tells your nervous system the threat has passed. My favorite is box breathing. Sitting down, with a straight back, breathe through the nose for four seconds (making sure to feel the belly expand, not just the chest rise) and exhale for six seconds. Do six sets.

---

**4. Get Your STORY RIGHT:** What story are you telling yourself?

Backstage, the story I was telling myself was *I was an embarrassment*. But that simply wasn't true. So, I wrote the story down in my journal. The lies, the doubts, the declarations—I put them on paper, closed the journal, and put it in my backpack.

Then I left it there.

What I replaced it with was simpler: I was willing to be the man in the arena. Not perfect. Not undefeated. Present. Competing. Refusing to be defined by one moment.

Are you rehearsing untruths or dealing in reality? Are you focused on what you can't control or what you can?

Perspective shapes performance.

**Get Right Practice:** Name your fears or emotions out loud, and write them down. What you can name, you can examine. What you can examine, you can change.

---

**5. Get Your CONFIDENCE Right:** Did you prepare like a champion?

Backstage my mantra became: *the reps, the reps, the reps.*

That was it. I had put in the reps and earned my spot. I had put in the reps and had everything I needed. I put in the reps and the work was already done. The only thing left was to compete.

Can you trust your preparation and step into the moment? Confidence isn't about the competition—it's about you and your work.

**Get Right Practice:** Recite a list of the specific work you have done to prepare for a moment like this—not outcomes, not titles, but actual preparation. Let the work speak louder than the doubt.

■ ■ ■

None of these areas operate independently. A shift in one tends to influence the others. Together, they turn a knee-jerk, fearful reaction into an intentional response. And can be the difference between staying stuck in a moment and moving through it.

There won't be a single moment where everything becomes clear or easy again. Backstage at the Arnold Classic, it was a series of smaller adjustments—a question asked, a journal closed, a shirt untucked, a pair of shoes changed, three words repeated like a mantra being chanted: *the reps, the reps, the reps*.

I adjusted my posture—not because it would change the previous lift, but because it influenced how I would operate moving into the next one. I interrupted the thoughts that weren't helping, not by pretending they weren't there, but by refusing to accept them without question.

I returned to what I knew was true.

The work had been done. The preparation was real. The opportunity to compete was still in front of me.

As I prepared for the next event, I focused on what was required in that moment—the feel of the bar, the positioning of my hands, the sequence of the lift. Not as a way to escape what had happened, but as a way to fully engage with what was next.

Nothing about the situation had become easier.

But my relationship to it had changed.

And that was enough.

In the next two events, I hit personal records, on the biggest stage, 30 minutes after my biggest failure.

That didn't happen because I suddenly became stronger than I had been before—but because I was able to change how I saw my circumstances. Yes, it was a hard situation, but it wasn't a bad situation.

The first lift did not define the competition.

My response to it did.

■ ■ ■

Moments like my experience at the Arnold Classic do not only exist in competition.

They show up in different shapes and forms, in different environments all across our lives: Something does not go the way you expected. A plan falls short. An outcome does not match the effort you put in. Life "jukes" when you "jive" and you are left to pick up the pieces.

How you respond in those moments, and the millions like them, shape more than individual outcomes.

They shape your character.

It's in those moments your beliefs are revealed, and your behaviors are pressure tested. Adversity does not ask for your résumé. It does not evaluate your intentions. It simply reveals the truth about you in that moment.

And the people who hold this uncommon belief—who have examined it, practiced it, and allowed it to govern their response when everything in them wants to step back—those people don't just recover faster.

They go further.

Not because of what happens to them.

But because of what they believe about what happens to them: *Hard isn't bad.*

## The Pressure Test

Think about the last time something didn't go the way you expected.

Not a small thing. Something you had prepared for. Something that mattered. The thing you got wrong. The job you didn't land. The conversation that went sideways. The week that fell apart inside an hour.

Now go back to the moments right after that adversity showed up unannounced.

What was the first story you told yourself? Not the version you would say out loud later, after you'd had time to compose yourself. The first one—the one that arrived before you could edit it.

1. Which choice did you make first: blame someone, make an excuse, or accept responsibility?

2. How long did it take before you started building the case for why it shouldn't have happened?
3. Did you compare your situation or result to someone else's, and how did that comparison influence your thoughts, words, feelings, and actions?
4. If you went back in a time machine to that exact moment, knowing what you know now, would you react the same? If not, what will you do to make sure you don't make the same mistake twice?

CHAPTER

# 6

# Optimism Requires No Evidence

> I choose optimism—not because the outcome is certain, but because certainty was never mine to control. What I can always control is my attitude, my effort, and my preparation, and I refuse to give anything less than my best.

In 2017, my friend James asked me a question that would change my life: "What would you do if you knew it would work?"

Simple enough, right? People get asked versions of that question all the time. It's the kind of dream-big, believe-in-yourself question that sounds inspiring in theory and feels terrifying in practice.

I'm a go-big-or-go-big kind of person, so I answered big.

I said I would take what I was doing as a volunteer at my local high school and do it for every school in Texas—and then the country. I would help one million athletes and coaches connect the dots between sports and life.

At the time, I had absolutely no evidence I could do it.

I had never started a business. I had no formal curriculum development experience. I didn't know video editing or graphic design. I didn't know how to lay out a PDF workbook, build a website, design marketing funnels, or create a sales strategy. I had never sold anything in my life. And I knew exactly two current head coaches.

Two.

Meanwhile, I was the breadwinner for a growing family—two kids under five and a third on the way. We had just bought a house. I had a stable job I had spent 10 years building: graduate school, long hours, credibility earned brick by brick.

Life was good. Safe. Predictable.

The rational voice in my head had a pretty compelling argument: *You're good for your local school. You don't need the big leagues. Don't lose a good thing chasing something unrealistic. You don't have what it takes to scale this.*

The evidence agreed with that voice.

There was no spreadsheet suggesting this would work. No investor backing the vision. No résumé that screamed, "This is the guy to do what has never been done."

Just a question.

*What would you do if you knew it would work?*

■ ■ ■

How would you answer that question?

What would you do if you knew it would work?

What happens in your body when you hear that question? Does your stomach tighten or your brain start racing?

When I ask people this question two things happen at the same time: First, I can feel the collective eye-roll of the crowd.

*Here we go. Cue the motivational speaker playbook. I bet the next thing he says is, "You can do ANYTHING"!*

And second: I see their *reasonable excuses* lining up to tell me why they, in fact, can't do *the thing*.

*It's irresponsible! I have obligations, bills, and a family to take care of.*

*I would love to chase my dreams, but I can't afford to take this risk.*

*What if I fail? How will I face my family, my friends, and most of all, myself?*

Now let me ask you another question: What would you say if I told you that I agree with you?

It is irresponsible to take a risk without counting the cost. It is rare that people live their dream.

You might fail.

The question James asked me, and I asked you, carries a false premise—*if you knew it would work*.

You never know. Not in advance.

Life and leadership don't offer certainty in the present tense. Relationships don't offer guarantees before vulnerability. Growth doesn't promise results before work or even after it.

Certainty lives in the past.

Which means every time you stand at the edge of something that matters—a new season, a hard conversation, a decision that could go either way—you are standing in a moment when certainty is not available.

And in that moment you have a choice.

■ ■ ■

The heart of James's question to me was never about certainty, or what I would do *if I knew it would work*. It was about the choice I was going to make in response to it.

How much authority do I give the evidence to decide what I will do, how I will do it, and most importantly who I will become in the process?

Sitting in my living room, across from James, the evidence was overwhelming. There were a thousand reasons I was not the person to do this.

And.

Something about letting things outside my control govern how I lived and operated in life didn't sit right with me. It was like sandpaper on my soul.

Though I didn't have words for it then, I now call this *evidence-based optimism*.

This is when we let external factors dictate our internal beliefs about how we show up to life's moments, big and small.

Evidence-based optimism says:

*When the evidence is in my favor, I'll take the risk—but it's not really a risk, because I've calculated it and I know I won't lose.*

*When the evidence is in my favor, I'll take the step of faith—but it's not really a step of faith, because I know the place I'm setting my foot will hold.*

*When I have evidence-based optimism, I know I won't fail—because I got the answers to the test before I ever took it.*

Make no mistake: This is comfortable, reasonable, and even responsible.

And something about it doesn't sit right with me.

■ ■ ■

My discomfort wasn't found in an aversion to comfort or responsibility, but in being governed by something outside of my control.

When the evidence said, "You aren't the guy for the job," I found myself pushing back and asking, *Why not?*

When the evidence said, "You don't have the right credentials to build a curriculum," I countered with, *But what if I was curious enough to learn to build a curriculum?*

When I first began meeting with coaches about the program, I had very little to show. Luke filmed and edited a video for me, and I put together a janky website and a black-and-white PDF workbook that broke every design rule I didn't know existed.

After I finished the presentation, a predictable pattern began to emerge. The coach would ask me a series of questions that all centered on one thought: "Does your program have this?"

And whatever the "this" was I would always answer the same: "Yes!"

Then, I'd write down, *Add this to the program.*

When it came time to market the program, the evidence told me I lacked the public relations chops to get it done. I wondered what if I could be a friend that served coaches, and not just a celebrity they followed. James encouraged me to start a podcast, not so that I could build a viral presence, but so I could build relationships with coaches.

My very first podcast was with a coach named Randy Jackson.

He had just put out a book called, *Culture Defeats Strategy* and he was as eager to talk about it as I was to learn about it. After the interview, he asked if I was open on Monday to speak with his team.

I told him I was open every Monday!

When Monday came, I asked an assistant coach if he would be willing to hold my iPhone and record the talk. Afterwards, I went to Starbucks and Googled how to edit videos on iMovie. I edited the video in three different styles, so it looked like I had been in three different places and started dripping them out to my meager Twitter following.

Every single coach that would like the video (which was only five or six), I sent a direct message and thanked them for the encouragement and offered to come share with their team. Coaches are always looking for speakers to motivate their team, and they asked how much I would charge them. I debated over this for a really long time.

I remember sitting at a different Starbucks (I'm a creature of habit) editing video the first time a coach reached out through my website to bring me in to speak. I went through 40 oz. of Pike Place debating what to charge: The evidence said I needed to establish the market early and get every dollar possible.

Good intentions don't pay the bills.

But as I thought about who I wanted to be, and the relationship I wanted to build with coaches, I found the answer to be something I would brand as "Gas and Gear" talks.

If you could pay for my gas and hook me up with some Nike, Under Armour, or Adidas team gear (I love Jesus, but I still have standards), I'd be there.

Over the next year, I'd give over 300 "Gas and Gear" talks, and drive over 60,000 miles across the state of Texas. I'd routinely drive 12 hours round trip for a 20-minute talk.

I became so obsessed with being a friend and partner to coaches that I missed the very real cost I was paying.

About a year in, things were moving fast enough to need more staff, more investment, and more people than I had money for. Half of the staff were working on IOUs and I lived on a repeating two-week countdown to find money before the next payday.

If I could profit from two nickels speaking to your team I would be there. So much so that when our third child was about to be born, I remember asking my wife to not have him on a specific day because I had booked an event that was actually paying me a speaker's fee to be there.

In a twisted misreading of what the Cycle was telling me was true about me, I remember actually being proud that I was that committed to the work.

That was not the first or last time my drive to prove the evidence wrong would cause conflict at home. But it wasn't just a conflict at home.

It was a conflict inside of me.

There is a real cost to allowing the evidence to dictate what you believe; you forfeit control of your attitude, effort, and choice. You stay at the mercy of what the evidence says should be true of you.

There is also a real cost to pursuing a dream.

I was in a hotel in Abilene, Texas, on a speaking tour that had me speaking 49 times in 48 days, when my wife called me in tears and told me that she missed me, and the kids missed me. She confessed that it felt like our loving relationship had transformed into a transaction: She cared for the kids and I paid the bills.

It wasn't what either of us wanted.

The evidence, it seemed, had spoken. The gambit was up.

And.

I felt the sandpaper on my soul again.

But this time, it wasn't the feeling of being controlled by some external verdict. It was the discomfort that I was stuck in an Integrity Gap of my own making.

It was entirely true that this wasn't what we wanted. I didn't want to be absent from my family.

And.

I wanted to have an impact on coaches and athletes through 2Words more than anything I had ever wanted in my life.

It would be dishonest to tell you that what happened next was born of me seeing the light and accepting everything the Cycle had revealed to me. If I am more honest than is comfortable, there was a healthy dose of "desperate attempt to hold everything together just a little bit longer" driving the decision.

When I finally got home from Abilene, I pitched my wife on the craziest idea that I had pitched her yet: that we sell everything we own, buy an RV, and travel together.

Where I was, they would be, too.

This was as crazy as it sounds. Not only would it mean that we would have to sell the nicest house either of us had ever lived in, and leave friends that we had come to love, but it would mean that we would have to homeschool our kids on the road, and contain three kids, an 80 pound goldendoodle, and everything we owned in a 44-foot box on wheels.

Oh, and we had never been in an RV.

For three and a half years we lived full-time on the road.

Leaky poop tanks, busted tires, and a longing for some personal space were regular occurrences. So were great adventures, lifelong memories, and outrageous experiences. We started our journey with three kids; we finished with four. Our fourth child was welcomed home to Yogi's Jellystone campground at three hours old.

What started as a desperate attempt to hold my family and my dream together became one of the sweetest times of our lives. So sweet, in fact, that I didn't have to wrestle with the still very real reality that, when left unexamined, my drive tended to push work over family.

That's the danger of success.

Then COVID hit.

Not only did we have to navigate quarantine from a 44-foot trailer but we also had to answer the question: How does our business survive?

The lockdown hit with about 10 weeks of school left.

The Texas High School Coaches Association asked if we would be willing to share a few video lessons with coaches to help them connect with their student athletes virtually.

The evidence said now is not the time to give your product away for free. Now is the time to pivot and figure out how to get money. Now is the time to hold on to the things that make you money and get as much as you can for it.

But that wasn't who I wanted to be, and it wasn't who I wanted us as a company to be.

I had said from the beginning that we were going to be a friend to coaches. If we bailed on them now, that would be a betrayal of all the work we had put in to become that friend.

We committed to sharing 10 weeks of lessons, doing a weekly encouragement message for coaches, and doing a Zoom meeting with any team that wanted it, for free. I did 60 from the front porch of my RV.

That fall, we waived the price of the curriculum for any school that wanted it, but couldn't afford it.

The skeptic would say, "That's just brilliant marketing."

Maybe.

But at the time, it was just the answer to the question, What would you do if you knew it would work?

I had no way of knowing what would happen when I answered that question the first time, or any time after that. No one can.

And that's the point.

■ ■ ■

I learned the phrase "Optimism requires no evidence" from Hall of Famer, and friend, Sue Enquist.

As a kid, Sue was never picked first.

She wasn't the biggest, the strongest, or the smartest. She read from the "special books" in elementary school. In high school, an academic counselor told her point-blank that she would never make it at UCLA.

But Sue had some sandpaper on her soul.

Despite her counselor's assessment, she made it to UCLA and exceeded every prediction. She was a member of the Bruins' first national championship softball team. Her 0.401 career batting average stood as the school record for more than two decades. She earned a gold medal at the 1978 World Championship with the US national softball team.

Her coaching career was even more remarkable. Eleven national championships—more than anyone in Division I softball history. Sixty-five All-Americans. Twelve Olympians. A 0.835 winning percentage across 27 years. Six halls of fame.

And then, after her softball coaching career ended, she was added to the staff of the 2020 US Women's Olympic Volleyball Team. Not softball—volleyball. A sport she had never coached professionally.

She wasn't brought in for volleyball skills. She was brought in for culture. She gave everyone a voice. She built accountability into a group of all-stars with big personalities who had never played together regularly. She centered belief where doubt had been living.

The result: The United States won its first-ever gold medal in women's volleyball.

"Her contributions to the team were the biggest asset," said four-time Olympian Jordan Larson.

Sue didn't transfer tactics to that volleyball team.

She transferred optimism.

## The Uncommon Belief

**Optimism requires no evidence.** I choose optimism—not because the outcome is certain, but because certainty was never mine to control. Who I am becoming is more important than what happens.

---

Optimism is more than a glass-half-full worldview.

It goes beyond cheap positivity and limp hope, and offers both a standard by which to measure yourself and a filter through which to understand the things happening around you.

*Merriam-Webster Dictionary* defines optimism as "an inclination to put the most favorable construction upon actions and events or to anticipate the best possible outcome."

When I read that, I read, "Find the best possible spin for the circumstances around you."

No wonder optimism is greeted with an eye roll.

The problem with this way of thinking is obvious: spinning the narrative on a situation doesn't do anything to transform you; at best it adds a spoonful of sugar to the bitter medicine life has offered you, and at worst gaslights you into thinking you just aren't "positive" enough for things to work out your way.

I see optimism as more than a lens through which to process information or a mental leaning. I see it as an action. A conscious choice you make, moment by moment about what you are going to do, how you are going to show up, and, most importantly, who you are going to become in the process.

I define optimism like this: *Optimism is engaging with any moment in life or leadership with alignment, conviction, and an add-my-best work ethic.*

Each element matters if you want to grasp how much this belief shapes your life.

**Alignment:** Closed Integrity Gaps. Make sure there is agreement between your declarations and your practice.

**Conviction:** Passion. Energy. Juice. A sense of want-to.

**Add-my-best positivity:** Ask the question *What's my best right now?* and give it to whatever is in front of you.

So when we choose optimism, this is what we are choosing: Alignment. Conviction. Add-my-best work ethic.

Do you see how much more compelling this understanding of optimism is? Why it can be both a safe harbor in a storm and wind in your sails to pursue your biggest goals?

Do you also see how this understanding of optimism costs you much more than the glass-half-full option? It demands you decide, before you know how the moment will play out, what you are going to bring to the table, if what you are bringing is aligned with your character, and if you are giving your best to it.

This demand is not unreasonable.

Optimism is a pre-decision about who you will be before the results are final, not a prediction about what will happen.

That pre-decision—deciding who you are going to be regardless of what comes your way—is the single most defining element of this uncommon belief.

Optimism, then, is not a stance toward outcomes. It is a stance toward yourself. You can change your plan a thousand times and remain optimistic. You can let go of one dream and pursue another and remain optimistic. You can fail at something—genuinely, completely fail—and still be optimistic.

Because optimism was never about the result. It was always about you.

■ ■ ■

Evidence-based optimism misses the mark because it tries to calculate and predict the future, as if certainty were the variable to solve for.

The uncommon belief doesn't solve for certainty, because that only lives in the past. Optimism, as I am defining it, solves for the present. It is a right-here, right-now equation.

Who are you going to be right now?

And if you repeat that decision over and over again, what is the Cycle going to reveal to be true of you?

I wonder if our fear of that answer is why we crave certainty—why the pressure test of uncertainty is so scary.

Not only do we want to know what will happen but we also want to know if we will like the version of ourselves that we will be when we get there. The irony, of course, is that who we become is a result of the choices we make right here, right now.

I know it can feel backwards to shift your focus from outcomes to development in the face of uncertainty, but releasing the need for certainty before action is not recklessness.

It is clarity about what is in your control and what isn't.

Optimism doesn't change your circumstances. But it can change how you show up, what you do, and who you become through those circumstances.

■ ■ ■

On a night in late August 2002, Coach Steve Roberts stood in a locker room after one of the most humiliating losses of his career.

His team had just been beaten 63 to 7 on national television in his first game as head coach.

The game wasn't even close. They were out-talented, outplayed, and outmatched. By every external measure the evidence had delivered its verdict on the rest of their season—loudly, publicly, in front of the entire football world.

Evidence-based optimism doesn't just waver in a moment like that. It collapses. It has every right to.

But even in a moment like that, Coach Roberts had a choice.

He could let the evidence set his posture. He could let the scoreboard speak for him. He could acknowledge the reality of what had just happened and let that acknowledgment become the ceiling on what his team believed was possible.

Instead, he chose something no one expected.

In the awkward silence of the locker room, where players knelt with both body and pride bruised, he declared, "We'll never have a better opportunity than this to prove that we are who we say we are."

Coach Roberts had some sandpaper on his soul.

Notice what he did and didn't do.

He didn't reach for a motivational match to light the flame of hope. He didn't make a hot take, bold prediction. He engaged with the humiliation that had just been handed to him. He didn't run from it. He welcomed it.

He looked hard in the mirror of reality and saw that if he didn't make a decision about how he was going to show up to this moment, the moment would decide for him. He had conviction. He added his best.

And all of this was decided before he knew how the season would end. Before he knew how the next game would go.

He didn't know what the season would produce. He couldn't. Not only was certainty not available but also the evidence didn't support his decision. But he had decided—in the worst possible moment, on the biggest possible stage—who he was going to be regardless of what the outcome turned out to be.

That is what it means to be more concerned with who you are becoming than what happens.

Not the refusal to acknowledge difficulty. The refusal to let difficulty set the ceiling on how he showed up, what he did, and who he became.

What followed was not magic. It was the belief made visible through daily work. The team came back. The culture changed. The program built something the opening night score had said was impossible. Three years later they stood at the top of their conference.

The 63–7 loss did not define the program.

The pre-decision made in that locker room did.

## The Three Commitments of Optimism

Choosing optimism once is a decision. Keeping it when the pressure tests come is a practice. You will fine-tune your own practices as you pursue optimism, but the following are three commitments that help me live out this uncommon belief.

### Stay Curious About the Unknown

The central conflict of the pressure test of uncertainty is that not knowing is a problem. And problems must be solved.

But uncertainty can't be solved for. The future is unknowable and uncontrollable.

And until you really look that truth in the eyes and accept it, you will continue to struggle with this pressure test.

Now, contrast that with the posture of curiosity.

Through the lens of curiosity, not knowing is no longer a problem, but a feature. The curiosity about what could be drives you forward to discover, not solve. Every unknown is another opportunity to explore.

This was my life blood in the early days of 2Words. Not knowing what coaches needed or wanted in a curriculum wasn't a problem because curiosity led me to ask questions and stay humble. I was eager to learn, never afraid to admit what I didn't know, and confident in my decision that whatever may come, I was becoming the kind of person who could serve coaches at the level I dreamed.

One way you can help develop the posture of curiosity is to practice what I call the *Rule of Six*.

The Rule of Six says that in the face of an unknown write down six possible answers to the unknown in front of you. They can be your best guess or your biggest fear. They don't need to be plausible—in fact, what you will find is that once you get past reason three, the answers naturally get more and more ridiculous.

And that is a good thing.

The goal isn't to solve the unknown. It's to remind yourself that you don't have to. When you don't know, the move is to stay curious—and stay focused on who you're becoming while you find out.

## Stay Faithful to the Pre-Decision

Your optimism will be tested. When it is, the question that you will be bludgeoned with is this: What's more important—process or evidence?

Who you are becoming or what the evidence is saying?

We all experienced this during the COVID lockdowns. And what we collectively found is that no amount of willpower could make the world well. We couldn't wish or hope things back to the way they were.

But we don't need to be in a pandemic to experience the pressure test of uncertainty. Life gives us that chance daily. Sometimes multiple times a day.

*This is life. These are its terms. What are you going to do about it?*

The struggle of optimism isn't to be so stubborn to your pre-decision that you change the current of evidence. It is to get out of the current of evidence all together. The evidence is going to be what it is. Stop trying to fight it. Instead, fight for your pre-decision.

That fight can look like giving thanks that the pressure test of uncertainty has given you the opportunity to be who you said you were going to be. It can look like finding mentors or those who are a little further down the path than you are, and spending time with them, learning from their wisdom and failures. And still other times, that fight can look like sitting honestly with the pre-decision—naming the cost, admitting the doubt—and then, eyes open, choosing it again.

Staying faithful to a pre-decision isn't about finding the right answer; it is about locking onto the process of who you are becoming, not the ebb and flow of evidence.

## Don't Let Success Mute the Cycle

If you really knew me, you would know that of the seven uncommon beliefs in this book, *optimism requires no evidence* is the one I am best at.

For me, the fact that I don't need to know what will happen in order to choose how I am going to show up, what I will do, or who I will become in the process is both freeing and energizing.

I also know that in my gold there is also shadow. My greatest strength is also my greatest weakness.

When you get good at something like optimism, or anything for that matter, the temptation will be to allow the success to mute the truths that the Cycle reveals. It's the danger of success.

The evidence that my relentless optimism produced about becoming the kind of person that helps coaches and student athletes gave me an excuse to turn down the volume on the cost of my optimism. I had conviction and add-my-best in spades; what success hid from me was that I'd lost alignment.

By the time we moved into the RV, my unwillingness to see what the Cycle was revealing—my tendency to prioritize work over family—was so fixed that I took the fact that we were together *all the time* as evidence that I solved the problem.

A few years later, that "solved problem" would prove itself very *unsolved* at the San Antonio airport.

Just like we can't let evidence dictate how we show up, what we do, or who we become, we can't let evidence keep us from doing the honest work of looking the Cycle in the eyes.

The way you do that, as we will look at more closely in Chapter 7, is to daily examine your life.

■ ■ ■

I don't see evidence as a bad thing.

It makes sense that evidence will begin to stack in one direction or the other, even if you pre-decide how you are going to show up, what you are going to do, and who you want to become.

The challenge—and this really is hard—is to not let that evidence control the thing that is yours alone to control: who you are becoming.

That's why the more I think about James's question, the more I realize just how brilliant it is.

*What would you do if you knew it would work?*

If I could defy reality and somehow know what would work, what I would come to know isn't an outcome or a strategy—not the awards gained or the goals reached. What I would come to know is the kind of person that I would have to become to reach that goal.

And even if I knew that, I would still have to make a choice.

I would have to daily, moment by moment, choose to show up with alignment, conviction, and an add-my-best work ethic. I would have to choose how I was going to show up every day, what I would do, and who I was becoming.

I would still have to choose optimism.

## The Pressure Test

Think about something in your life right now where the evidence isn't moving the way you wanted it to.

The season that started slow. The relationship that's plateaued. The project that's not landing. The team that hasn't bought in yet.

Now look at how you've been showing up to it this week.

Not how you talked about it. Not the version of yourself you presented in the meeting. How you actually showed up—your attitude, your effort, your preparation—in the hours when no one was watching.

1. How much of your best are you giving it right now?
2. Have you actually made a pre-decision about who you are going to be in this, or are you still negotiating your posture with the scoreboard?
3. Who are you becoming through the process, and is that the person you want to be on the other side of it?
4. Who pays the price when you leave your Integrity Gap open?

# CHAPTER 7

# I Am Not My Performance

I refuse to allow something that can be taken from me to be my foundation. I will pursue daily the examined life.

The stewardess gave me an apologetic smile as she extended the tray my way.

"I'm sorry, sir, the only meal we have left is our vegetarian option."

Worse words had never been uttered.

Sensing my disappointment, she went in search of anything with protein. She came back empty-handed.

Growing up and well into adulthood, the only vegetables I ate were potatoes, corn, and chicken—and apparently not all of those even qualify as vegetables. I had never eaten a salad in my life. There wasn't technically one on my breakfast tray, but the absence of meat told my brain I was flirting dangerously close to breaking a lifelong streak.

But hunger is hunger and calories are calories.

So I ate.

And to my great surprise—it wasn't that bad. I mean, it wasn't good. But it wasn't that bad.

As I worked my way through the terminal in search of real food, I called my wife and told her what had happened.

"I really did it. I mean, it wasn't that bad. I bet I could go vegan or whatever they call it."

She laughed out loud.

"You, go vegan? You think chicken is a vegetable. You had me go through the food line twice at the wedding this weekend—asking for chicken and beef—so nobody would catch you going back for thirds. There is no way. You can't do it."

Four words.

*You can't do it.*

Challenge accepted.

Cold turkey. No questions asked.

For five years.

■ ■ ■

On the surface it was simple. Don't eat meat. One decision that answered a thousand smaller ones.

But it was one of the hardest things I have ever done—because there was another layer to the story.

Yes, I went vegan because my wife said I couldn't. But that was more the straw that broke the camel's back than the real reason.

The real reason is that I had been wrestling with something much deeper.

At 6′1″ and 330 pounds, I was almost always the biggest and strongest person in any room I walked into. I could do cartoonish feats of strength—overhead press 405 pounds, bench press 500 pounds, bend steel bars, rip a deck of cards in half with my bare hands.

But I struggled—really struggled—to go up the stairs to play with my kids. Getting down on the ground wasn't something I did. I was big enough and strong enough to pick up a house. I just couldn't run around it.

Something had to change.

But here was the problem: I believed—genuinely believed—that if I weighed less than 290 pounds, nobody would listen to me speak.

## Performance-Based Identity

Looking back, that statement sounds as ridiculous to me as it probably does to you. But in the moment, the fear was as real as anything I have ever felt.

It wasn't just a question of how I would pay the bills. My size wasn't just a physical reality—it was the answer I had been giving to a question I didn't know I was asking.

Who am I?

And when you start answering that question with something as fragile as your size, your marketability, your influence—things that can all be taken away—it's only a matter of time before they are.

I didn't know it then, but what I was living had a name.

Dr. Benjamin Houltberg calls it *performance-based identity*—the belief that who you are is defined by what you do.[1] That your identity, value, and worth live inside your performance. That when the performance moves, you move with it.

You've seen it if you have ever spent any time around teenagers: it's the roller coaster they ride. High and confident one moment, full of self-doubt the next. Performing beyond their abilities on Tuesday, looking for a way out of competition on Thursday. Most people chalk it up to emotions, but it's something deeper than that. It's a crisis of being.

When someone finds their identity in their performance, competition stops being about fun or development. It becomes a measure of worth. That's why so many want to quit when things get hard—not because they're afraid of competition, but because they're afraid of what losing might say about them.

Losing a game means they're a loser. Making a mistake means they are a mistake. Failing means they are a failure.

It's harder to see in adults—or maybe just harder for us to admit—but we ride the same roller coaster. We tie our identity to job titles, paychecks, social standing, how well our kids perform, what someone said—or didn't say—after they visited our home. We allow things that could be taken away in a heartbeat to define us. And while we may not always recognize the identity judgments we're making, we understand the fragility completely.

One of the hardest things I have watched is what happens to people in my community when they retire without a purpose plan. They had a financial plan. The golf membership. The fishing boat. The RV. But once those things lost their luster, they started to lose themselves in who they used to be. They used to be respected. They used to make decisions that mattered. People knew them. Now the thing their lives revolved around for 40 years is gone, and they don't know who they are anymore.

This is why career-driven parents struggle to step away from work. Why do we take the loss of a deal so personally? Why does our anxiety spike every time the boss calls? When you find your identity in what you do, anything that threatens your ability to do it becomes a threat to who you are and what you are worth.

When I ask high-performing student athletes what they are most afraid of, the answer is almost always the same: failure.

When I asked Hannah—a 4.0 student on her way to a Power Four program, with every service hour, character recommendation, and civic award you could imagine—she said this:

> *"It feels like failure makes my work worthless. And if my work is worthless, what does that make me?"*

That is performance-based identity in a single sentence.

Who I am and what I do have become so connected that a loss in sport makes me a loser in life.

I believe this is the single greatest challenge most people don't even know they are facing.

It was the challenge of a lifetime for me.

And I found a way out.

■ ■ ■

What going vegan offered me was a chance to step off a roller coaster I didn't know I was riding.

For the first time, I had to examine a belief I had never questioned.

Was it actually true that if I lost the weight—if I got as small as 290 pounds—no one would listen to me speak? Was I less of a leader, less of a man, because I wrestled back control from something that had stopped serving me and started running me? Could it be true that I was more than my size?

As I learned to eat differently, I learned something else entirely. My foundation had been hijacked. And as the weight came off—past 290, all the way down to 240—I found out that the reason people listened to me had nothing to do with how much I weighed. The examination freed me to ask a better question: If I am not my size, who am I?

What matters most to me? What is the anchor of my life? What do I serve that is bigger than me?

I can't answer those questions for you. They are yours to examine and yours to name. But I can tell you what I found when I asked them myself: my faith, my character, and my calling.

Three things that cannot be taken from me. I can walk away from them. I can neglect them. But no outside event can snatch them away.

This is what Dr. Houltberg calls moving from performance-based identity to purpose-based identity—shifting the answer to "who am I?" from what you do to who you are beneath the doing. Connecting to something bigger than yourself. Refusing to let the highs and lows of life set the terms of your worth.

I knew these things mattered. I had taught them. I believed them.

But because I had stopped examining my beliefs, I missed what was happening underneath them. The very things meant to express my faith, my character, and my calling had quietly climbed into the seat those things were supposed to occupy.

Which brought me to the hardest lesson of all.

Moving from performance-based identity to purpose-based identity is not the same as living a purpose-based identity.

■ ■ ■

"Welcome! Card please?"

I flashed my executive membership card and gained access into the members-only warehouse. It was family Costco day, and we were having a blast.

Aisle by aisle, we went. Not in a hurry. Not looking for anything in particular. Just knowing that if we were meant to have it, Costco would lead us to it—and it would come in a 48-pack.

We were somewhere just before the turn—that moment where you hit cookies and the walk-in freezer, just before you bank to the meat section and work your way up the other side—when it hit me.

An overwhelming desire for a Costco hotdog.

In five years of being vegan, nothing had tempted me to break. Nothing except a Costco hotdog.

I can't explain it. Maybe I don't need to. Costco hotdogs speak for themselves—a quarter pound at a time, with a drink, for $1.50 since 1985.

What happened next felt less like a conscious choice and more like something came over me. I told my family I needed to use the restroom. Then I made my way to the Costco café. I thought about backing out—just ordering a drink—but before I had fully decided anything, I had ordered a hotdog, covered it in mustard and onions, and eaten the first meat I had consumed in five years.

It was perfect.

The bun, toasted just right. The mustard, sharp and tangy. The onions. The quarter pound of all-American beef that had been waiting for me to return to it for five long years.

For about 60 seconds, it was the best decision I had ever made.

And then the spiral began.

*Vegans don't eat hotdogs.*

What have I done? Someone is going to see me. The cashier knows. I am going to be found out. Five years of stories and teaching moments and bloodwork and credibility—and I am standing in the Costco café with mustard on my beard like a fraud.

I was terrified.

So I did what anyone would do in that situation. I checked my phone—selfie mode—to make sure there was no mustard in my beard. Then I walked back to my family without saying a word.

I've said it before, but I'll say it again: Looking back, that statement sounds as ridiculous to me as it probably does to you. But in the moment, the fear was as real as anything I have ever felt.

The very thing that had helped me step away from performance-based identity had become its own performance prison. Going vegan helped me shift from defining my identity, value, and worth by my size to my faith, character, and calling. It had given me great stories to tell, powerful teaching moments, superior bloodwork, and a lean-in credibility that made people's eyes go wide when they found out I didn't eat meat.

It made me feel healthy, whole, in alignment.

Which is why somewhere along the way, I stopped examining it.

I missed how it had unintentionally become a different variation of what I had left five years before.

This is the hidden danger of learning the difference between performance-based identity and purpose-based identity. You can start to believe that once you make the shift, the work is done.

It isn't.

■ ■ ■

## The Uncommon Belief

**I am not my performance.** I refuse to allow something that can be taken from me to be my foundation. I will pursue daily the examined life.

---

The riptide of performance is strong.

The satisfaction of developing new skills. The praise of people. The pride of being the first, the only, the best. There is nothing wrong with any of those things when they stay in their lane and do their job.

Performance isn't bad. It just isn't stable enough to build your life on. That was never its job.

That's the job of purpose.

Which raises a fair question: What is purpose?

Cards on the table—I can't answer that for you either. It's a little like love. You can define it one way or a thousand different ways, but you will know it when you find it. What I can tell you is what it has to be capable of doing, because not everything that feels like purpose actually is.

Purpose is bigger than you. It extends beyond your own advancement, comfort, or recognition. It is oriented outward toward something or someone that would exist and matter even if you were no longer the one serving it.

Purpose cannot be taken away. A title can be taken. A role can end. A season can close. Purpose is not attached to any of those things. It is the conviction underneath them, and convictions don't get handed back when the job does.

Purpose results in the good of another. This is the test. If the thing you are living for only benefits you, it is a goal. When it reaches beyond you—into the lives of the people you lead, raise, serve, or simply share space with—it has the weight of something worth building on.

You will answer the question of purpose differently than I will. That is the point. You don't need my purpose. I don't need yours. But we both need one—something examined, something named, something we have looked at honestly enough to trust when the performance stops cooperating.

That is what it means to say I am not my performance.

Not that performance doesn't matter. Not that winning is irrelevant or that results are beside the point. It means that when the results are gone—when the season ends, when the role changes, when the scoreboard goes dark—you still know who you are. Because you built on something the scoreboard never had access to.

I'll show you what that looks like for me.

When I have to look myself face to face and get honest—not about my accomplishments or my failures but about who I actually am—I go to three places:

- **My faith.** I follow the Way of Jesus. This is the foundation of my life. My ethos, my actions, my values—they all begin here. It is not a set of rules I maintain or a performance I keep up. It is the way of being that I have submitted my life to. You cannot take that from me because I did not earn it and I cannot lose it by failing to perform.

- **My character.** In Chapter 3 we defined character as the pattern of beliefs and behaviors that consistently guide how you show up in life's hardest moments. This is foundational for me. My character has been built through choices no one watched and decisions that cost something real. It is not my reputation—what others see. It is what the Cycle reveals when the pressure is on and no one is keeping score.
- **My calling.** This is where my faith and my work come to life. I feel called to help raise up the next generation of leaders. How I do that is secondary. Right now it is vocational—it is the work of 2Words. But it could be how I volunteer, where I give my time and resources, what I show up for without being asked. That is what makes it untakable. I could lose the business tomorrow. You still could not steal the calling. It does not live in the job title. It lives in me.

More than my occupation. More than my accomplishments. More than my failures.

This is the truth of who I am.

I refuse to let something that can be taken away be my foundation. And when I am tempted—when the riptide pulls and the scoreboard starts talking—I know exactly where to go.

Not to my last performance.

To these three anchors.

■ ■ ■

Knowing what cannot be taken is not the same as living from it.

My vegan experience proved that. I named my foundation. I made the shift from performance to purpose. And still performance found its way back to the driver's seat—not dramatically, not all at once, but the way you misspell a name in an important email, miss the turn to your house, or take your eye off the ball at exactly the wrong moment. You are fully capable of not doing any of those things. But you got distracted. Complacent. Overwhelmed. Or you simply stopped looking.

Different reasons. Same outcome.

Sometimes it's a simple lapse. Sometimes it's a refusal to see what the cycle is already revealing. Sometimes it's not looking at all. But knowing the right foundation and living from it are two different things—and the distance between them is where the work actually lives.

Think back to how Aristotle described habituation, the process of building character.

We don't become courageous by thinking about courage. We become courageous by doing courageous things—repeatedly, deliberately, until courage stops being something we reach for and starts being something we return to. Virtue isn't a gift. It isn't a personality trait you either have or don't. It is built through repeated action and the slow accumulation of choices that eventually become who you are.

We become what we repeatedly do.

Foundation works the same way.

You don't have a foundation by naming it once. You don't have it by making the shift from performance to purpose and calling the work finished. You have it by returning to it—daily, honestly, without waiting for a crisis to make the return feel urgent—until the return becomes who you are.

That is the examined life.

It is not a list of rules. It is not a legalistic burden. It is not a retreat you attend once a year or someone else's 37-step morning routine reposted from LinkedIn.

It is this: looking honestly and intently at your actions, your patterns, your beliefs, and your character and asking whether they are in alignment with your purpose. Not as a verdict. Not as a judgment. As a statement of reality. A plain reckoning with what is actually true, followed by a choice about who you want to be and what you want to be defined by.

Day by day. Moment by moment.

That is what makes it a practice. Do it once and it is just an act. Do it daily and it becomes who you are.

"I will daily pursue the examined life" is not inspiration. It is the operational commitment that makes this belief real. Without it, "I am not my performance" is a slogan. "I refuse to allow something that can be taken from me to be my foundation" is immature overconfidence. The daily practice is what turns both of them into something you can actually stand on when the pressure arrives and life gets hard.

The Cycle has one job. It reveals what is actually true—not what you intend, not what you declared, but what your patterns show when the pressure is real. If the Cycle keeps showing performance, performance is what's driving you. No amount of protest changes that.

The examined life is what keeps you honest enough to see it.

And to do something about it.

## A Daily Examination

The central claim of this book, that character is the ultimate competitive advantage, hinges on your willingness to "do something about it."

Every belief we'll examine—every refusal, every posture, every commitment—either rests on your willingness to be more than your performance or collapses into it.

*Hard isn't bad* becomes a coping strategy if you can't find yourself in adversity.

*Optimism* becomes a performance if you don't know who you are.

*The hard truth* we are going to discuss next becomes a threat if your identity can't hold what it reveals. And after that: Mastery, relationship, service all require a foundation stable enough to see the truth of the Cycle, and do something about it.

Let's talk about how to examine yourself, and make sure you are living from purpose not performance. Not only on your best days, but on a terrible Tuesday in April.

### Morning: Keep Performance in the Passenger Seat

The morning examination happens before the day starts pulling on you.

It is less a pregame speech and more a declaration: a centering on what matters most before you go and do anything. It is also an assigning of seats. Purpose in the driver's seat. Performance in the passenger seat. Roles clear before the day starts.

When seats are assigned before anything happens, both purpose and performance can do their jobs. Performance can push you toward excellence. It just can't tell you who you are.

Three things worth anchoring before your day begins:

- **What is my foundation?** Affirm the purpose you have named for yourself. Remind yourself why it matters most. This is the unglamorous work behind the cliché—the main thing is to keep the main thing the main thing. Say it out loud if you have to. The morning is not the time to assume you remember.
- **How would I act if my foundation dictated my actions today?** Stop concerning yourself with outcomes for a moment. Ask how your foundation requires you to show up, regardless of results. You cannot always control the win. You can always control the alignment.
- **Where am I most likely to take my eyes off purpose and put them on performance?** You are the expert on you. You know where the riptide pulls hardest. Name it before it happens. Call it out while the day is still quiet. It is significantly easier to refuse a lie you have already anticipated than one that arrives without warning.

What this looks like will be different for everyone. For me it is the morning office from the Book of Common Prayer, a time of scripture and prayer that centers me on what matters most before anything else gets a vote. For you it might be a journal, a walk, a committed time of silence. The specific discipline is not what matters. What matters is the practice of anchoring yourself to your foundation before the day begins making its demands.

Before a big meeting or competition it might look like a photo of your family or a quiet moment of gratitude for the opportunity in front of you. Before starting toward a new goal it might look like clearly distinguishing between what is a performance outcome and what is a purpose-driven reason to pursue it.

Whatever shape it takes, make sure purpose is in the driver's seat before you put the car in gear.

■ ■ ■

## Midday: Notice, Name, Refuse

Mike Tyson said everyone has a plan until they get punched in the face.

The morning is when you make your plan. The middle is when you get punched.

Throughout the day—in the middle of a hard conversation, a big meeting, a competition, or just the ordinary wear and tear of a Tuesday—the lies begin to arrive. The pull of performance gets stronger. The cost of staying true to yourself turns out to be more than you had budgeted for. A piece of feedback lands like a verdict. A comparison starts to pull. A win tempts you to build on it. A loss tempts you to answer with it.

When that happens, three verbs.

**Notice it.** Don't react. Don't skip to solving a problem that may not exist. Instead: See it. Feel it. Let the doubt or the fear or the pull be present for a moment without immediately doing anything about it. The Cycle reveals character. The pull of performance reveals what you haven't yet thought to examine. See it before you move.

**Name it.** Give what you are noticing a name. This is something I learned from my friend and mentor Jim Placio. When something as abstract as fear or doubt shows up, it can be hard to get hold of. Sometimes it is just a whisper, a vague unease that doesn't announce itself clearly. When you name it, you turn the light on in the closet where you thought the monster was hiding. You see what you are actually dealing with instead of reacting to what you imagined.

I have an internal critic that never quite shuts up. It starts out sounding helpful: asking reasonable questions, checking my work, making sure I mean what I say. But if I'm not careful I'll follow the current of its questions right into an accusation I didn't see coming. Its favorite is fraud. *You aren't that good. You're a big fish in a small pond. Once people get close enough they'll see the truth. I'm going to catch you.*

I named this voice Officer MIA—My Internal Affairs Officer. When Officer MIA gets loud, I notice. I give her space.

Sometimes she sees something I don't. But what I don't give her is control. That is not her job.

**Refuse it.** You cannot keep performance from wanting to take the wheel. That is what it does. What you can do is refuse to hand it over. Look at the pull directly and say, "Thank you for wanting to help, but that is not your seat." Then return to your foundation and keep moving.

■ ■ ■

## Evening: Audit Your Wins and Losses

At the end of the day, look back.

Not to relitigate what happened but to examine what it belonged to.

Performance win? Name it. Enjoy it. Don't let it climb into the foundation seat overnight.

Performance loss? Name it. Learn from it. Don't let it become a verdict by morning.

Purpose alignment? Celebrate it—not as a result but as formation. You are becoming who you said you wanted to be.

Purpose drift? Notice it honestly. Return tomorrow.

This can happen in a journal or in a conversation with someone close enough to tell you the truth. The format is not what matters. The honesty is.

■ ■ ■

I will pursue daily the examined life.

Not because it guarantees you will never drift. You will. The riptide pulls. Performance finds its way back to the driver's seat in ways you didn't see coming and couldn't have predicted on your best morning.

The examined life doesn't promise you won't lose control of the wheel.

It offers a way to find your way back.

That is the confidence the morning practice builds—not that today will go perfectly, but that when it doesn't, you know where to return. That is what the midday practice protects—not that the lies won't arrive, but that you have learned to notice them before they name you. That is what the evening audit produces—not a perfect record, but an honest one.

Here is what I have found to be true after years of doing this work—in my own life and in the lives of the people I have had the privilege of watching do it well.

When you know who you are, you don't have to prove who you are.

When you know who you are—not what you have done, not what you have earned, not what the last performance said about you—you don't have to spend your days auditioning. You don't have to win to feel worthy. You don't have to outrun the fear of being exposed. You don't have to check your beard for mustard and hope nobody noticed.

You already know. And knowing is enough.

But you only know who you are by examining your life. Not once. Not at the beginning of a new year or the launch of a new goal. On a random Tuesday in April, in the grind, when no one is watching and nothing is at stake except the accumulation of who you are becoming.

The people who hold steady when everything the scoreboard measures gets taken—they are not stronger than you. They are not more talented or more disciplined or more gifted with certainty. They simply know something you now know, too. That their worth was never on the scoreboard. That the foundation underneath them was built before the performance began and will remain long after it ends.

They are not their performance.

Neither are you.

## The Pressure Test

Think about how you present yourself to people.

The leader. The parent. The athlete. The one with values everyone has heard you talk about, foundations everyone has heard you name, the principled stands they have seen you take.

Now think about last Tuesday.

Not Sunday morning. Not when you were well rested and ready for the week. A regular Tuesday—somewhere between coffee and lunch, in a moment no one was watching.

Who showed up?

The person you present or someone else?

Did the person who showed up on Tuesday make a quiet decision—to look at a phone, to skip a conversation, to take the easier road, to eat the metaphorical hotdog—that the version other people see would never have made?

This is the test. Not whether you have a foundation, but whether you live from it on a Tuesday in April when nothing is at stake and no one is watching.

1. What did you do, in private, that you would not have done if someone you respected was in the room?
2. What did you say out loud about your foundation that was less about anchoring yourself and more about signaling the values you have?
3. When the Cycle revealed an Integrity Gap this week, did you examine it or did you check the mirror to make sure no one could see the "mustard in your beard"?
4. How do you personally separate who you are from what you do?

## Note

1. Benjamin Houltberg, "Playing with Purpose: Athletic Identity and Relationships in Sports." *Search Institute Blog*.

CHAPTER

# 8

# The Truth Is Not My Enemy

I will always receive hard truths, have hard conversations, and pursue the truth—even when it is uncomfortable.

Pathetic.

That's how I felt. And how I looked.

The guys heckled me from the third floor window. "To the left!" one of them shouted. "Your other left, dummy!" said another.

Snow invaded my untied boots and soaked my socks. Freezing cold and burning hot at the same time.

*How did I get here?*

Simple. In a fit of frustration I threw my chemistry book out of the window of my dorm. Then, in humiliating defeat, I walked down the stairs, out the front doors, and through the snow to the back of the building. I was left to dig my chemistry book out of the snow in the middle of January.

Between my curses I mumbled about how unfair things were, and how this shouldn't be happening. And yet, it was. Despite my football potential, my leadership, influence, and aptitude for the military, I couldn't escape the simple fact that if I didn't pass the chemistry test the next day, I would be sent home from the United States Air Force Academy Prep School.

A failure.

Never in a thousand years did I think I would be sent home. I was supposed to be the kid who beat the odds. Instead I became the kid who proved them right. To play football at the Division 1 level, earn a college degree from one of the most prestigious universities in the world, and serve my country—just as my father had done in the greatest air force on the planet. It would have been the ultimate all-American story.

And I was one test away from throwing it all away—and having to pay to replace a snow-soaked textbook.

■ ■ ■

There was no singular moment when my dream burst into glorious flame. It wasn't when the commander told me

I was done or when the head football coach chewed me out for being a disappointment to (in this order) God, my country, my family, my coaches, my teammates, and least important of all, myself.

My failure happened slowly, and then all at once.

It wasn't like the staff there didn't try. I had tutors, study hours, every resource the Academy could throw at me. The problem wasn't access. It was me.

I was unwilling.

Unwilling to lock in during class or study at night. Unwilling to ask for help.

Unwilling to hear the hard truth that if they couldn't trust me with chemistry, they couldn't trust me to lead in battle.

What happened to me at the Academy wasn't a deficiency in my intellectual ability.

It was the result of ignoring what the Cycle was telling me.

My lips said that I valued education, leadership, and the opportunity to be at the Academy. My life demonstrated a very different pattern.

That pattern didn't end at the Academy. For years afterward, my move was the same: If someone challenged me in an area where I was strong, I could hear it. If they challenged me where I was truly deficient, I had a hundred ways to shift the conversation back to what I was good at.

It looked like self-awareness. It was evasion.

And I am not the only one who avoided hard truths.

## Four Ways to Refuse Truth

The confrontation of truth is never comfortable. It hurts when your spouse says something at dinner you didn't want to hear and you spend the drive to work the next morning building a case for why they are wrong. It's embarrassing when you snap at your kids in public or lose a game or deal you had no business losing. I get why comments from your parents are like fingernails on the chalkboard of your soul and why you haven't talked to them in six months.

When the truth hits, it can feel like an attack. Like rejection. Like the person delivering it and the words themselves are both against you.

It's threatening.

And when something feels threatening, we do what humans have always done: We fight it, run from it, freeze, or appease our way out of it. But the truth isn't a predator. It's not here to hurt you. Yet, most of us have spent years learning how to keep it at arm's length, and we've gotten so good at it we don't even notice we're doing it.

Here are four teaching stories to help you see what it looks like.

### Redirect

I am a master at deflecting truth and turning the conversation toward something I am great at. I'll say things like, "Look at the growth. Look at what we've built. Look at all the good we're doing."

I redirected a hard truth a volunteer tried to share with me in my first leadership position, and I still cringe when I think about it.

Steve was giving his time—freely—to help me run a nonprofit. He came to me one day, hat in hand, and told me he felt disconnected. That he didn't feel included in what we were building. That he wasn't sure he was even needed.

He was vulnerable enough to say that out loud. To his leader.

And I heard him. I really did. And then I explained, with great confidence, why he was wrong.

The mission is too important to slow down, I told him. Look at our growth. Look at everything we're accomplishing. We can't let people who can't keep up set the pace.

"I don't have time to hold your hand."

I thought I was being honest. I thought I was protecting something worth protecting.

When he quit the next week, I told myself he just wasn't cut out for it.

Never once did I stop to consider that maybe *the problem was me*.

That's what a redirect of a hard truth will do.

## Weaponize

Mark was a local pastor. Attendance was up. Donations were up. The church was growing and he had the spreadsheets to prove it. He wore that growth like armor. But when his elder board sat him down and told him they were concerned about the irreverence he'd been showing and the way he'd been treating people behind closed doors, things changed.

He came to the next meeting with a bullet list.

Not to listen. To argue. And when he ran out of counterarguments, he turned the whole thing around and accused them of creating division. Suddenly the men who loved him enough to tell him the truth were the problem. The confrontation became evidence of their disloyalty instead of evidence of his blind spot.

He didn't just refuse the truth. He weaponized it against the people who delivered it.

### Minimize

I knew a guy named Vince. He was a small business owner who had earned his success the hard way: brick by brick.

But when he heard things he didn't like, he had a nasty habit of making them smaller.

Like when his chief financial officer (CFO) started noticing expenses that didn't add up. Personal charges bleeding into business accounts—technically legal but not standard practice. Small ones at first—easy to explain, easy to dismiss. She'd bring them up and he'd wave her off with explanations, delivered with just enough confidence to make her feel like it would be okay.

But as cash flow slowed faster than expenses, his explanations got thinner. And she got genuinely uncomfortable. But he'd look her in the eye and tell her she was worrying over nothing.

By the end of the year the business was short on cash. He came to her frustrated, looking for answers.

He didn't reject the truth. He just minimized it—one paper-thin explanation at a time.

## Excuse

Debbie was the kind of boss you'd run through a wall for.

Generous. Loyal. The type to remember your kid's name and buy the whole team dinner just because it was a hard week. You wanted to work for her. You wanted to make her proud.

But when something would go wrong she would flip a switch.

She could tear you apart with precision. Not yelling exactly—something worse. Cold. Targeted. The kind of words that follow you home and sit on your chest at 2 a.m. And then the next morning she'd be back—warm, generous, like nothing happened. The pendulum would swing and you were supposed to swing with it.

When people close to her finally said something—"Hey, this isn't okay, the way you talk to people when you're angry isn't okay"—she didn't fight it. She didn't attack them for bringing it up.

She just shrugged.

"That's just how I am. I'm intense."

She turned a behavior into an identity—and once it was who she was, there was nothing left to correct.

Four people. Four tactics. Redirect. Weaponize. Minimize. Excuse.

Not one of them thought they were avoiding the truth. I thought I was protecting the mission. Mark thought he was defending against division. Vince thought the expenses genuinely weren't a big deal. Debbie thought she was just being honest about who she was.

Every single tactic felt completely reasonable to the person doing it, and they all four missed a truth that was genuinely for them.

That's what makes them costly.

## The Uncommon Belief

**The truth is not my enemy.** I will always receive hard truths, have hard conversations, and pursue the truth, even when it is uncomfortable.

---

The truth is not out to get you.

When presented with the reality of your beliefs, actions, or character you are not being served a prison sentence.

You are being given a choice.

A choice between receiving the truth or rejecting it. Paying the cost of growth or the consequence of your fear.

We have seen the costs of not receiving the truth: lost opportunity, broken trust, and compromised integrity. Choosing to ignore the truth will always bring consequences, and they will often hurt. That's not to say that receiving the truth is easy—just the opposite. It is uncomfortable to hear, hard to wrestle with, and annoyingly persistent.

That's why it is so uncommon.

■ ■ ■

## How to Receive Hard Truths

The truth is a competitive advantage.

How? The direction of truth is forward. It will never hold you down or pull you back. Truth moves you toward growth.

Think back to the story of Debbie.

Her team was committed. They were willing to run through a brick wall for her. When they confronted her with the truth about her behavior, and how she talked to and treated them, they weren't looking for Debbie to make things easier; they wanted her to grow as a leader, treat them with respect, so that they could do more! Seeing the truth as a threat held Debbie in place.

We will never grow past a truth we aren't willing to hear.

Here's how to receive the hard truths.

■ ■ ■

### Ask: How Is This True?

That one question can transform truth from a dagger to a scalpel.

I learned this from my friend and mentor Jim Placio, who taught me to be curious about feedback instead of wary of it.

When we start with "Is this true?" we position ourselves to debate, deflect, or deny. When we are willing to ask "How is this true?" something important happens: We let go of the need to be right, which opens us up to hearing the feedback.

Consider Mark.

When confronted with the feedback from the church elders about his irreverence and how he treated people behind closed doors, he went from "Is this true?" to "It isn't true!" to "They are attacking me!" in rapid succession. Had he started with the flip, he might have come to a different conclusion.

"How is it true that I am being irreverent?" could have led to "I never considered how someone from a different generation would interpret this."

"How is it true that I didn't treat people with respect?" might have revealed "I can sometimes run over people with my passion."

The point isn't that every piece of feedback you get is right—it's not, and we'll address this next. The point is that when you are curious enough to consider the possibility that it is true, your body and mind operate from a place of curiosity, not threat.

The next time feedback comes your way:

Slow.

Down.

Wait two seconds longer to respond than feels natural. Give the knee-jerk reaction of "Is it true?" space to pass, then flip the script and ask, "How is it true?"

You will be surprised what you find.

### Filter: Preference, Principle, or Practical?

Not all feedback deserves the same weight.

This is where a lot of people get stuck. They either treat every piece of feedback like gospel—collapsing under the weight of everyone's opinions—or they dismiss it all as noise and reject it all. Neither works.

You need a filter.

When feedback comes your way, run it through three questions.

**Is This a Preference?** Preference is someone's opinion. Their taste. Their way of doing things.

It might be valid. It might even be helpful. But it doesn't carry the same authority as a standard or rule. A friend thinks you should have called instead of texted. Someone thinks you should have handled the conversation differently. A colleague wishes you'd given more context before diving in. Your boss would have written the email differently.

Hear it. Weigh it. But don't let it own you.

Preference-based feedback is information, not instruction. You get to decide what to do with it.

**Is This a Principle?** Principles are different.

Principle isn't someone's opinion—it's a shared standard. A value. An expectation that exists beyond any one person's wants or desires.

*You were dishonest. You treated someone with disrespect. You fell short of the standard.*

When feedback is rooted in principle, the filter has already answered the questions, "Is this true?" and "How is this true?" This doesn't get debated. It demands action.

The common mistake is treating principle like preference—running it through their feelings, negotiating with it, waiting to see how they feel in a few days.

That's not discernment.

That's avoidance.

**Is This Practical?** Once you've decided the feedback is worth acting on, you have to get honest about one more thing: *Can I actually do this?*

Not *Do I want to?* Not *Do I agree with it?* But—is my Integrity Gap a matter of *will* or *skill*?

Because those are two different problems that require two different solutions.

A skill gap means you genuinely don't know how. You need training, coaching, a model to follow. That's not weakness—that's just an honest assessment. Get help.

A will gap means you know what to do. You just haven't decided to do it yet.

And this is where your favorite threat response tactics can hold you back.

*I don't know how to have that conversation.* Do you not know how, or have you just decided it isn't worth the discomfort?

*I'm not sure what the right move is.* Are you genuinely unclear, or are you clear and scared?

This was me at the Academy. The Integrity Gap was never skill, access, or support. I knew exactly what was required of me. I had all the resources in the world. The problem was my unwillingness to do the work to learn.

I blamed everyone and everything except the one thing that was actually causing the problem.

Me.

## Take: Three Steps Forward

You got curious.

You ran the filter.

Now it's time to do the work.

Here's what most people get wrong about change: They think it has to be dramatic. A complete overhaul. A new person starting on Monday. So, when they can't pull that off, they conclude they aren't capable of changing at all.

That's not how it works.

You are never more than three steps away from a change.

**Step 1: Name What Isn't Helpful** You already know what this is. The deflection. The minimizing. The pivot to blaming another. The sarcasm that ends the conversation before it starts.

You don't have to fix it yet. You just have to name it.

Out loud.

*My minimizer is really loud right now.*

*I can feel myself deflecting.*

*That response I just gave—that was me getting defensive.*

That's it. That's Step 1.

Think about Vince. His instinct when his CFO raised concerns about their expenditures was to minimize her. To explain it away. To make her concern the problem instead of the spending.

A Step 1 for Vince isn't fixing the budget. It's catching himself mid-minimize and saying, "Actually—I can see how what I just said might make you feel like I'm not taking this seriously."

That one sentence changes the course of the conversation.

Naming it out loud does two things: It interrupts the pattern and it signals to the other person that you are actually in the room. Present. Willing.

Don't underestimate how much that matters.

**Step 2: Start Doing What Is Helpful** The goal here isn't to solve the problem. It isn't to be radically different in a single moment.

It's direction.

Are you moving toward growth—a new understanding, a better perspective, an honest look at a blind spot—or are you moving away from discomfort?

Those are the only two directions.

For Vince, Step 2 sounds like this: "Can you help me understand why you see things differently?"

That's it. One question. But notice what it does. It turns a confrontation into a conversation. His CFO can now share her concerns instead of defending them. Vince gets a window into what could have been a costly blind spot. And the relationship moves forward instead of calcifying.

You don't need a breakthrough. You need a step.

Ask one honest question. Sit with the answer a beat longer than feels comfortable. Let someone finish a sentence you want to interrupt.

That's Step 2. Direction over destination.

**Step 3: When You Want to Quit, Go Just a Little Bit More** The further down this road you go, the harder it gets.

At first it feels exciting. Novel. You're growing, you can feel it, the feedback is landing and you're responding well and you think, *I think I've got this.*

That's the easy stage. Low-hanging fruit.

Then it keeps coming.

More feedback. More truth. More gap between who you are and who you're capable of being. And somewhere in there, a voice shows up that sounds reasonable but isn't.

*I've already grown so much. How much more do they want?*

*No matter what I do, it's never enough.*

*At some point this becomes nitpicking.*

*I think people are taking advantage of my openness.*

Don't fall into that trap.

That voice isn't wisdom. It's ego, looking for an exit ramp.

Because here's the thing about growth: It doesn't get easier, you just get better at receiving it. And the better you get at it, the harder the feedback gets. Why? Because the people around you trust you more, expect more, and see more in you than they could see before, so they offer more to you.

The feedback increase isn't a sign that you're failing.

It's a sign that you're worth investing in.

So when you're ready to quit—ask one more question. Get curious one more time. Take one more step toward the truth instead of away from it.

That's the *do*.

Not perfection. Not transformation overnight.

Just one more step forward than you took yesterday.

## How to Have Hard Conversations

Until now, the flow of truth has been outside in. From others to you.

But if we are going to believe that truth is not our enemy, then we need to make it a two-way street—we must be willing to have hard conversations and share hard truths.

This is easier said than done.

But just like we make a posture shift from "the truth is out to get me" to "the truth is for me," we can make a posture shift about sharing the truth. Hard conversations don't have to be destructive.

Here are what I call the Three Ts of a having a hard conversation.

### Be Tactful

Not everyone hears the truth the same way.

That's not an excuse to soften it—it's a reason to be smart about how you deliver it.

Tactful doesn't mean gentle. It means strategic. It means you know who's sitting across from you before you open your mouth. Some people need connection first. They need to feel known before they can be challenged. The harder the truth, the more relational currency you need in the bank.

Some people need detail. Give them the full picture. Let them process. That's not coddling—that's respect. Some people just want the path forward. Skip the long conversation. Tell them what needs to change and why it's the better road.

Tactful is simple: Know your audience before you speak.

## Be Truthful

Truthfulness is where most leaders flinch. They want to be kind, so they start softening. They start hedging. They start wrapping the hard thing in so much cushion that the person walks away thinking everything's fine. That's not kindness. That's cowardice wearing a "kindness costume."

Truthful means being direct and kind—at the same time, not one or the other. It means complete. Nothing left out. Nothing buried in the footnotes hoping they won't find it. And it means no false hope. If something has to change, say it like something has to change. The person sitting across from you deserves a clear picture, not a comfortable one.

### Be Committed to Teaching

Teaching is the motive check. Before you say a word, ask yourself, *Why am I doing this?*

Because if you're calling someone out to make yourself feel powerful, to prove a point, to win an argument—stop. That's not a hard conversation. That's a Trojan horse attack.

Real teaching comes from real care. You have to want the person to grow more than you want to be right. You have to be invested in what comes after the conversation, not just the conversation itself. If you care enough to call them out, you have to care enough to help them make it right. That's the litmus test.

That's what separates accountability from cruelty.

■ ■ ■

Most people avoid hard conversations because they're afraid of the reaction. And I get it. Nobody wants to be the one who makes someone cry, or gets shut out, or starts a conflict that didn't exist before.

But here's what I've learned: The conversation you're avoiding is usually the one that matters most.

And hard conversations don't get easier with time.

The longer you wait, the more the problem gets bigger, louder, and harder to fix. Hard conversations, done well, are one of the most loving things you can do for another person. Those conversations say, "I see you. I believe you're capable of more. And I care enough not to pretend otherwise."

## Pursue the Truth

There is a third posture when it comes to making truth more than an enemy: pursuing it.

Not waiting for it to find you or confront you, but seeking it out. Treating it like the treasure of all treasures.

I love how the late Eugene Peterson, author of *The Message*, translates Proverbs 15:14:

> *"An intelligent person is always eager to take in more truth; fools feed on fast-food fads and fancies."*

How much has trading the richness of a hard truth for a cheap drive-thru snack cost me? How much has it cost you?

But that is the beauty of the Cycle. It doesn't judge you or deliver a final sentence. It just reveals. And the reality is that the Cycle has revealed times in our lives where we were unwilling to hear the truth. But even that truth can move us forward. It's kind of like this:

As of this writing, I am 40 years old. Multiply that by 365—I've been alive roughly 14,600 days. And if you average out my meals over that stretch, I've eaten somewhere around 65,700 meals.

Of those 65,700 meals, I only remember a handful. Riley's BBQ and homemade Arnold Palmers at my wedding. My buddy Luke's open-flame ribeye steak at deer camp. Every Perry's seven-finger pork chop. The first time I walked into Gibson's Steakhouse in Chicago with my friend and mentor Brad Black.

A handful. Out of 65,700.

And yet—every single one of those meals I don't remember kept me alive for the ones I do. There was a stirring inside me every day, multiple times a day. A hunger. A physical response to go find fuel. Some meals were healthy. Some were gas station tacos. But it took all of them to get me where I am today. I wouldn't be here without them.

Pursuing truth is like that.

Some days you take in just enough to get you to the next meal. A small correction. A quiet conviction. A moment of honest self-reflection that doesn't feel like much but keeps you moving. Other days, you ignore a truth you know you should receive, and indulge in your refusal tactic du jour. Then, there are the days you sit down to a truth that you will remember for the rest of your life—one that changes how you see yourself, how you lead, and how you love.

■ ■ ■

There is no pretty bow to put on my time from the Academy.

I was asked to leave because of my refusal to hear the truth. Then, in a government-defying act of God, I was given a second chance. And I blew it. Again.

I wish I could tell you there was a moment where this all clicked for me. But there was no singular moment. There was just day after day, meal after meal, where the Cycle gave me a chance to see the truth with fresh eyes. And over time, I began to see myself. I asked new questions, weighed what was before, and started moving forward.

One truth at a time.

And somewhere along the way, my appetite began to change. The cheap truth wasn't good enough anymore.

And now? I want the whole truth.

I'm hungry for it.

I wonder: How hungry are you?

## The Pressure Test

Think about the last time someone told you something hard about yourself.

Not feedback you asked for. Not the kind that confirmed something you already wanted to believe. The kind that landed somewhere it wasn't welcome—about a pattern, a blind spot, a way you've been treating someone, a place where your behavior doesn't match the leader you say you are.

Now go back to what you did with it.

Did you redirect—pivot the conversation back to something you were good at? Maybe you weaponized—turned it around and made the person delivering it the problem. Maybe you minimized—waved it off, explained it away. Maybe you excused—named it as just *who you are*.

But maybe you did the harder thing. You sat in it. You didn't deflect. You let the truth land.

Whatever your response, the question that matters most is this: Did anything change?

This is the test. Not how many turns the truth took to reach you, but what you did with it when it finally did.

1. Did the truth become action, or did you receive it well and quietly shelve it?

2. What hard conversation are you owing someone right now that you've been telling yourself you're "still thinking about"?
3. Who has stopped telling you the truth, not because you fought it, but because you received it well and nothing ever changed?
4. And how hungry are you for the whole truth?

CHAPTER

# 9

# Mastery Is Not the Destination

I refuse to arrive. I will always strive to be better today than I was yesterday because I am worth that work.

It started with an email from the head football coach of the University of Missouri: an invitation to come speak to the team in 13 days.

Saying yes to a speech has never been easier. This was the ultimate confirmation that the work I was putting in—hundreds of speeches, thousands of miles driven, and countless nights away—was finally paying off.

I was headed to speak to a Southeastern Conference football program.

When I rolled onto campus and began the facilities tour, it became crystal clear this place was built for one thing—developing elite football players—and it looked every bit the part.

The branding was elite. And the players matched the energy.

In the team room every player had their notebooks open. Pens out. Locked in. These were alpha competitors who treated the classroom the same way they treated the weight room and the film room: as another chance to find an edge. I loved every bit of it.

The room was buzzing with electric conversation. The head coach barked, "EYES!"

In unison the players responded, "EYES!" and a disciplined silence fell across the room. "What happens for the next 60 minutes," Coach declared, "Is as important as what we do on the field. We don't just want to build great players. We want to build great men."

I reached into the coin pocket of my jeans and pulled out my bottle of Northern Lights Black Spruce oil. I'm not a superstitious guy, but I am a little 'stitious.

Every great speech I had ever delivered began this way.

Dab the left wrist. Dab the right. Close the bottle. Swipe my wrist across my beard. This is what winning smelled like.

Coach finished his introduction. I stepped on stage.

■ ■ ■

I learned to be a speaker the way most professionals do: I learned a formula.

I gave my first speech in eighth grade, at a youth night at church. My mom helped me write it. I was so nervous I couldn't eat. But the moment I stepped on stage, something switched on inside me that I didn't know was there. I came alive in a way I hadn't known was possible. I loved it.

I spent the next decade chasing that feeling: speech clubs, student leadership, anything that put me in front of a room. But it wasn't until 2012 that I started doing it as a job. School assemblies. Faith-based events. The kind of apprentice-level work that teaches you to be a professional.

The training was simple. You needed three school assembly talks and five faith-based messages. They gave you the formulas. They gave you the models to follow. The goal wasn't to be a great teacher. The goal was to be able to give eight talks, automatically, and own the room, no matter how tired you were, no matter how long you'd been on the road. One of one. Flip the switch and go.

I got good at it. *Really* good at it.

But by the time I started 2Words, I didn't want to have eight talks anymore. I wanted to be a craftsman. This was my art, and I needed to find my voice.

So I studied the people I admired. Eric Thomas. Tony Robbins. Rick Warren. I developed a process. Find a speaker. Mimic them.

How they talked. How they dressed. What they talked about.

*Become* them, as completely as I could. Then evaluate. What felt natural? What felt forced? Keep what felt natural, drop what felt forced. Then find the next speaker and do it again.

Over the years, I'd put it all into a blender—what I'd kept from each one—and season it with my personality, my experiences, my context. And slowly, the feedback I'd receive started to change. People stopped saying, "You remind me of . . ." and started saying things like "I've never heard anyone explain it that way before." That was a marker. That was the moment I knew my voice had become mine.

It took me 18 years to find it. I'll spend the rest of my life fine-tuning it.

But by the time I got to Mizzou, there was one piece of my early formula I hadn't fully let go of: my story.

My story was the first thing I had ever learned to deliver well as a professional speaker. It was the safe, automatic, always-works close that I could reach for whenever the teaching felt thin. In the truest sense of the word, it was my silver bullet. The safe place that, if I could just get to it, I knew the speech would land.

I told it really well. And it worked. It did everything it was supposed to do, every time. But it had become an internal groan. Not because I didn't believe it. Because I wanted to go further, and I didn't trust myself to go further without it. *Could I trust my voice? Or was I crazy for trying to do something different?*

It was a mix of discontentment and longing. Fear and wondering. A pull I had been overriding for longer than I cared to admit.

When I built the Mizzou talk, I built it the way I wanted to. The teaching was mine, the structure was mine, the voice was mine. But I also teed it up so I could add the story at the end as an insurance policy. *I'm going to give you the real me.*

*But I'm going to keep the safety net within reach, just in case the real me isn't enough.*

That was the truth of it. The talk was always going to be the same. The only question was how I was going to end it. Was I willing to show them the full me—teaching voice and all—and trust it? Or did I need the rescue?

I was prepared to do it. I just didn't know if I would.

■ ■ ■

I stepped on stage and the energy was through the roof. I had to remind myself to slow down and breathe. I was all piss and vinegar back then—speed, volume, energy, crank it up—and Mizzou was a room that wanted all of it.

I was locked in. Not performing. *Teaching*. The slides were dialed in. I'd given the players expectations on the notes I wanted them to take. The teaching was hitting where I'd planned it to hit, and I could feel the room with me—that locked-in silence that tells you the work is landing.

But in the back of my mind, a question kept surfacing: *Are you going to tell the story?*

The feeling was similar to wanting to push your limits in just how far you could swim in a lake. You know the buoys you always turn around at—you can see the buoys ahead of you in the water—but the closer you get, the more you feel the pull to just keep going.

I kept teaching. The buoys kept getting closer.

And as I got near the place where the story would have entered, something quieter than I expected started speaking inside me. It wasn't a voice arguing with another voice. It wasn't fear and pride wrestling. It was something gentler than that. An assurance.

*You don't have anything to prove.*

*What you said is true. Good. Helpful. You gave them what they needed to take the next step in their journey. And you did it well.*

*Don't make it about the story.*

That voice didn't make the story the bad guy. The story wasn't the enemy. The story was a piece of the formula that had carried me for years and still worked. The voice wasn't asking me to hate it. It was just giving me permission to let it go. To trust the voice I had built. To trust that the teaching could stand on its own.

And right at that moment—the moment when the old script handed me off to the story, when the buoys were two strokes away—I scanned the room and locked eyes with Luke.

■ ■ ■

Luke has been a constant presence in my life since 2017. Every speech, every video, every lesson I have taught carries his fingerprints somewhere on it. Yes, he's the video guy. But calling Luke *the video guy* is a bit like saying Nolan Ryan played catch for a living. It's not wrong. It just misses the point.

Luke is my thought partner. An extension of my creative brain. No one in the world has heard more of my teaching than he has or has watched my development as a speaker in more detail. When we're filming, he doesn't just shoot. He listens. He looks for moments, watches for what's working and what isn't, giving me feedback in real time without ever taking the camera off target.

He has tells. When I land a point well or hit a phrase the way I'd been hoping to, he does this little head bob, like he's jamming to music. When I say something unexpected—or something wrong—he stands straight up behind the camera and gives me a look that only the two of us understand. These are the small, private exchanges that happen in every speech I give. The room has no idea Luke is doing any of it. The room sees a videographer floating across the back, grabbing different angles. But Luke and I are having a silent, second conversation.

So when I got to the moment in the speech where I would usually have said "What you don't know about me is, I was born to a teenage mother"—and I blew right past it—Luke popped up from behind the camera like Punxsutawney Phil looking for his shadow and gave me a full-toothed smile.

*I see you, Mack. Let's go.*

He knew what no one else in the room knew. I wasn't just closing my speech. I was trusting who I was becoming enough to drop the safety net. He knew I'd been wanting to do it—we had talked about it around and around. I just hadn't been clear on whether I would. I didn't want to mess Mizzou up. I didn't want to ruin the opportunity.

But I also knew I didn't want to be a robot.

That was the tension. And Luke—the only person in the room who could possibly have known what the moment meant—was standing in the back, grinning at me like he'd been waiting for it.

I grinned back.

I kept teaching.

When I walked off that stage I knew something about myself I hadn't known an hour earlier.

I was willing to move past the formula.

■ ■ ■

High performers love formulas.

We may give them different names in different industries—scripts, strategies, protocols, playbooks, systems, Google Docs shared across teams—but what they all ultimately do is what formulas were made to do. They give you a way to take specific inputs, run them through a known process, and get specific outputs. And not just any outputs.

The *right* outputs.

If high performers love anything more than formulas, it's the right answer.

We love knowing that if I do A + B, I will always get C. Because if I know that to be true, I am going to 10×, 12×, 100× my A + B so that I get even more Cs—specifically more Cs than you, and better Cs than you. That's what high performers do. We love formulas. We love checklists. We love step-by-step processes. Think about every leadership and self-help book you've ever read. They all have a big promise: Do *this* and get *that*.

Including the one you're reading right now.

The framework at the center of this book—belief shapes behavior, behavior practiced becomes pattern, pattern tested under pressure reveals character—can be read two ways. You can read it as a formula: Run the steps, produce the output, arrive at character, done.

Or you can read it as a cycle: The character revealed by one run becomes the belief that shapes the next run, and the Cycle never stops turning. The first reading ends somewhere. The second reading doesn't end at all.

Most high performers, by default, read it the first way. Not because they're lazy readers. Because that's what high performers do with frameworks. We turn them into formulas. We find the inputs, we run the process, and we reach for the output. It's how we've succeeded at everything else. It's the tool we trust. And the tool is genuinely helpful.

But the tool has a cost, and the cost is hard to see from the inside.

When you treat a framework as a formula, you unintentionally start treating its output as a destination. You start believing that character, growth, excellence—whatever the framework promised—is a place you can input your way into. Something you can plug the right pieces into and produce. Something you can *arrive at and master*.

And once you believe mastery is a place you can arrive at, you sacrifice the one thing you wanted most.

■ ■ ■

Think of it like this.

If you were to put "mastery" in your GPS, what would your app of choice give you?

The first thing you'd see is a map. Overlaid on the map is a line, and a clear set of directions: Turn right here. Exit there. Continue on the hard work tollway. But the most important information it would give is this: Estimated time of arrival: 10,000 hours.

Thanks, Malcolm Gladwell.

And what do you do once you arrive at your destination? You stop traveling. You unpack your bags and set up camp—fire pit, s'mores, tents, and all.

Three tents specifically: comfort, pride, and fear.

They are the shelters we pitch when mastery starts feeling like the destination, and leaving stops feeling like an option.

## The Three Tents

**Comfort is the tent you didn't mean to pitch.** Nobody sits down one morning and decides to stop growing. You just wake up inside a rhythm that works, look around, think, *This isn't so bad*, and stay. Not because you made a decision. Because the decision never got made. You got comfortable enough, for long enough, that the thought of leaving stopped occurring to you.

Comfort doesn't argue with you. It doesn't have to. It just makes the alternative feel like unnecessary trouble.

**Pride is the harder one to see, because pride is built out of real things.** Real sacrifice. Real successes. That's what makes it so hard to leave—it's not protecting a lie. It's protecting the story you've been telling yourself.

*I earned this. I built this. I paid for this with years I don't get back*.

Pride doesn't keep you stuck by telling you you're better than you are. It keeps you stuck by telling you that what you built deserves to be defended, and that reaching past it would dishonor the version of you who built it.

**Fear is the tent pitched right next to pride, but facing the opposite direction.** Pride protects the story you tell yourself. Fear protects the story you tell everyone else. It isn't worried about what you privately believe you're capable of—it's worried about what happens to the version of you other people believe in, if you reach for more and come up short.

Fear would rather you never find out.

So it hands you a reason to stay that sounds a lot like wisdom, and you take it, because the alternative—trying and failing—feels like too much to risk.

Three tents. Three different shapes of shelter. All of them built to keep you exactly where you are.

And all of them built *on top of* the same mistake: believing the formula had delivered you somewhere final. That the Cycle had done its work, produced its output, and handed you a thing to protect.

That belief is the common belief. The unexamined one. The one almost every high performer is carrying without naming.

And it's the belief that is costing you the edge you are seeking.

## The Uncommon Belief

**Mastery is not the destination.** I refuse to arrive. I will always strive to be better today than I was yesterday because I am worth that work.

---

I refuse to let mastery be the destination.

Not because I don't want to be a master of my craft. Just the opposite.

I want to be excellent. I want the work I produce to be the work other people in my field point to when they're trying to figure out what *good* looks like. Because I want to be the best at what I do, I refuse to let mastery be the end of the journey.

The belief I am asking you to consider is not "Don't pursue mastery." The belief is "Don't arrive."

Refusing to arrive is harder than it sounds, because almost everything in our lives is built to reward arrival. Promotions, titles, and praise all reward arrivals of one shape or another. The whole architecture of professional success is calibrated to the moment you finally *get there*—wherever *there* is for the role you're in. To refuse to arrive is to refuse the reward structure most people are organized on.

It's to keep walking past the moment everyone gives you permission to stop.

That kind of refusal needs a reason underneath it. Without one, it sounds like restlessness and ingratitude, and it mutates you into the kind of person who can never enjoy what they have because they're always reaching for the next thing.

The reason I want to keep going is simple but hard to deeply believe: *I am worth the work.*

Not *I will become worth it if I do the work*. Not *The future version of me is the reward and the work is the price*. Something more honest than that, and harder to say without it sounding like a slogan.

The person you are right now—the one who has done the work to get here, who has lived through what it took to arrive at this moment, who has paid the costs and made the choices and put in the reps that built the you that is reading this sentence—*that person* is worth the work that's still ahead.

Not *The work will produce a better version of me*. Maybe it will. Maybe it won't. You could hit a home run or you could swing and miss. The next thing you try might be the thing that transforms your life, or it might be the thing you never quite figure out, or it might be something else altogether. None of that is what makes you worth the work.

What makes you worth the work is *who you already are*. The work that's ahead of you is the appropriate response to the person you have already become. To stop reaching would not be a missed opportunity. It would be a betrayal of the years that built you, of the choices that shaped you, of every honest reach you have already made on the way to standing where you are standing right now.

That belief is the difference between a person who keeps growing and a person who settles. Not talent. Not discipline. Not an opportunity. *The conviction that who you already are is worth the work that is still ahead.*

Most of us don't believe this. Not really. Most of us believe we are worth the work *as long as it pays off.* As long as someone recognizes it. As long as it produces the version of us we were imagining when we started. We have it backwards. We treat the reward as what justifies the work, when actually *who we already are* is what justifies the work, and the reward—if it comes—is just a bonus on top of an obligation we already owed ourselves.

But when you get this right, something shifts inside you. The reach stops being about a future payoff and it becomes about *honoring the present.*

You don't reach because you're trying to become someone. You reach because you already are someone, and that someone deserves to be matched with continued effort. The next step isn't ambition. It's fidelity. Fidelity to the person you have already worked hard to become.

This is why pride, comfort, and fear are so hard to leave behind—and the cruel thing about them is that they all, in their own way, claim to be protecting us. Pride claims to be protecting what I built. Comfort claims to be protecting my peace. Fear claims to be protecting my reputation. All three of them sound like they are on my side.

They aren't.

They are protecting *the version of you that has stopped becoming*. The shelters say, "We are keeping you safe." What they are actually doing is keeping you from the work you are worth.

Pride betrays you by refusing to let you grow past what you have already done.

Comfort betrays you by elevating your ease to the driver's seat.

Fear betrays you by deciding you are too fragile to risk for what is next.

All three of them pretend to protect you. They are actually saying *you are not worth the next step.*

That is the lie at the center of every tent. And it is the lie this belief refuses.

You are worth the next step. You have always been worth the next step. The work that is ahead of you is the appropriate response to the person you have become.

Refuse to arrive.

Because you are worth the work.

■ ■ ■

I keep talking about mastery as a destination, as a place. A point on a map. Somewhere you arrive after enough work, enough reps, enough years to show how it will let you down.

So what is the alternative to mastery? *I will always strive to be better today than I was yesterday.*

Or in a word: *growth*.

Try putting that in your GPS. Type *growth* into the destination bar and see what the app does. There is no pin to drop. There is no line to draw across the map. There is no estimated time of arrival, because there is nowhere to arrive. The app was built to get you to places, and growth is not a place.

Growth requires a compass.

Not the metaphorical kind but an actual compass: the kind you would hold in your hand, with a needle that points. A compass does not tell you how far. It does not tell you how long. It does not tell you when you will get there, because *there* is not part of the conversation. All a compass does is tell you which way you are facing.

Which means a compass can do something a GPS cannot. It can separate two things the GPS fuses together: motion and direction.

On a GPS, motion and direction are the same thing. If you are moving, you are moving toward the destination. If you stop, you stop making progress. The two are locked together because the whole system is built around arrival.

A compass breaks them apart. You can be moving fast and facing the wrong way. You can be standing still and facing exactly the right way. Motion does not prove you are growing, and stillness does not prove you are not. The only thing that matters—the only thing the compass will tell you—is the direction you are facing at any given moment.

And here is the uncomfortable part of the compass.

You can drift off course without meaning to.

A GPS will yell at you when you go off route. "Recalculating. Make a U-turn." A compass says nothing. The needle just moves, and if you are not checking it, you will not know. You will keep walking. You will feel productive. You will look around at the ground you have covered and assume that because you are tired, you must be getting somewhere. And you might be. Just not where you thought you were going.

And the only way to know whether you are still facing it is to stop and check the needle.

## Checking the Needle

Checking the needle is the practice this whole chapter has been building toward.

It is not a step-by-step process. It is not a five-point framework. It is one question, asked honestly, asked often enough that the asking becomes a habit.

*Am I facing the right direction?*

That is the question. That is what checking the needle actually looks like. You stop, in the middle of whatever you are doing, and you ask whether the work you are doing is moving you in the right direction.

But be warned: There will be times you do a lot of really good work in the wrong direction. That answer is not a failure. It is the needle doing its job. The needle is *supposed* to show you when you have drifted.

When the needle tells you the truth, you do not get to argue with it. You do not get to negotiate. You get to do one thing, and one thing only: Choose to turn back toward the direction you said you were facing or pitch a tent.

Once the needle is pointing true and alignment is set, the work begins.

This is where everyone who has ever taken a leadership book seriously will recognize themselves, because this is the part the leadership genre talks about all the time. *Hard work. Discipline. Consistency. Showing up.* The part where you put your head down and grind. I am not going to spend much time here, because you already know how to do this part. You have been doing it your whole career. It is the part you are elite at.

But I will say this: Hard work that is not preceded by alignment is just motion. It is the GPS trap. It is moving fast in the wrong direction and feeling productive because the speedometer is climbing. The genre teaches hard work as if it were the answer to everything, and it is not. Hard work is the answer to *one* thing: covering ground in a direction you have already chosen. If the direction is wrong, the harder you work, the further you get from where you said you were going.

Alignment first. Then work.

In that order, every time.

■ ■ ■

Once you have checked the needle, and you have started doing the work, and you are walking hard in a direction you actually believe in, something will happen that the leadership genre does not prepare you for.

You will fall.

Not metaphorically. Not character-arc-of-the-chapter fall. *Actually fall.* You will reach for the next thing and miss. You will try the new teaching and watch it land flat. You will pitch the project and the room will not buy it. You will be visibly bad at something, in front of people who used to think of you as the person who was good at things. The fall will be real. The cost will be real. The embarrassment will be real.

And here is what the compass tells you about that fall that the GPS never could: A fall in the right direction is still alignment.

A confident walk in the wrong direction is still a drift.

Falling forward means falling on your face *with the needle still pointed at growth*. It means stumbling toward the version of you that is worth the work, instead of striding toward the version of you that is already on the shelf. The fall does not unalign you. The fall is *evidence* of alignment, because you only fall when you reach, and you only reach when you have decided that the person you already are is worth more than a stopping point.

There is real risk, but it is not that you will fall.

The risk is the moment you decide the fall hurts too much to be worth getting back up. The moment you decide that the safe road, the proven move, the comfort tent, the formula you already know—that those are good enough for you now. That you are not worth the next reach. That the next version of the work you might have done is not owed to the person you already are.

That is the only failure this belief is afraid of. Not the fall. The *deciding the fall was the end of it*.

If you can fall, get up, and keep walking in the right direction, you are still growing.

If you stop falling because you stopped reaching, you have arrived. And arrival, in this chapter, has only ever meant one thing: You stop growing.

■ ■ ■

I still think about taking the exit ramp sometimes. In every speech I have given since Mizzou, there is a moment when formula would have handed me off to the safe story—the story that always works, the story that was my training wheels for 15 years, the story I could have ridden into a comfortable career as a memorable speaker.

I do not know if it will ever stop appearing, and I am not sure I want it to.

Because every time it appears, I get to choose again.

I get to look across the room and find Luke, and I get to remember what I decided on a stage in Columbia, Missouri.

I get to remember the person who was standing on that stage—the one who had given 600 speeches to get there, who had spent 18 years finding his voice, who had walked into that team room and felt the dread of playing it safe one more time. I get to remember that person was worth the reach.

That I am still worth the reach.

So every time the exit ramp appears, I check the needle. And every time the needle is true, I walk past it.

Not because I have arrived.

Because I refuse to.

## The Pressure Test

Think about an area in your life that you want to be great at.

It can be in your work, your leadership, your relationships, or life in general.

Do your actions show that you have arrived or that you are arriving?

You would label yourself as *arrived* if you find yourself camped out. Not because you have decided to stop growing, but because you decided that where you are is good enough.

Maybe you reached and missed. You tried something past your level, fell on your face in front of people who saw it, and somewhere in the days that followed you decided the safer move was to go back to what worked. You didn't decide you had arrived. You just decided the fall wasn't worth getting up for.

Or do your actions show you are arriving?

That you aren't yet where you one day will be, but you are on your way. If you find yourself there, the most important question to answer is this: Why are you still pushing?

Are you hoping that a little bit more effort will get you to a better campsite? Or are you working because you believe the most uncommon of beliefs: that you are worth the work.

1. In what ways have you arrived? And in what ways are you arriving? Why do you think those differences exist?
2. What have you been calling contentment, or wisdom, or self-protection that is actually one of the three tents?
3. What did it cost you to get where you are—and is the way and why of how you are working honoring that cost?
4. What changes today if you stop treating the next reach as ambition and start treating it as fidelity to who you already are?

CHAPTER

# 10

# I Don't Have to Do It Alone

Independence is not strength. Asking for help is not a sign that something is wrong with me—it's how I show my strength.

I believe people want to be helpful.

Call me a dreamer.

Tell me I'm wrong, naive, or that my Texan is showing.

But everywhere I go, I see people joyfully being helpful.

Strangers holding the door open and smiling at strangers as they pass by. Volunteers delivering meals on wheels to the less fortunate or shut in. Friends going above and beyond for one another. I love to see it.

When was the last time you helped someone out?

If a friend—right now as you are reading this book—texted you and said, "So . . . listen. I'm at Taco Bell and I forgot my wallet. Can you Venmo me $20 so I can buy my lunch?" You might have questions—namely, how many Crunchwrap Supremes does one person need—but you would send the money. Right?

Of course.

What if a coworker or project partner came to you and said, "I am so behind. I thought phase one would take me two days—I'm going on a week! Can you help me catch up?" Would you help?

No doubt.

Saturday morning you're at home, watching College Game Day and prepping for the big game and your best friend calls you: "I was on my way to your house for the game, and I ran out of gas. Can you come get me?" What do you do?

You head into the garage, grab the gas can, and drive to the rescue.

And what about if late one Tuesday night you're up scrolling funny videos, trying to avoid the fact that you have to wake up way too early to be up this late, and a text pops up:

> *"I know it's late. And I am really sorry . . . but can you talk?"*

How do you reply?

You just hit the call button.
I believe people want to help.
So when was the last time you asked for help?

## Leadership Is Lonely

Call me crazy. Tell me I'm off base.

But for every person I see willing to help another, I see five who are unwilling to ask for help. And five more lining up their arguments for why they'd ask for help—they just don't need it.

What about you? Are you willing to ask for help?

I know the right answer. So do you. But the excuses are louder than the answer.

**Excuse:** *They're busy. I don't want to bother anyone. They have enough on their plate.*

This is the easiest go-to excuse because we tell ourselves we're actually doing them a service. We're helping them. And it's so much easier to protect them from being overwhelmed than it is to admit we are.

**Excuse:** *I should be able to handle this. It's not that big a deal. What would they think if they saw I couldn't handle a task this small?*

This plays into pride. It doesn't matter how small the task actually is. The size of the task isn't the point. The point is the story we'd have to tell about ourselves if we asked.

**Excuse:** *If I ask for help, people will think something is wrong with me.*

This is the one that handcuffs us the most. If I tell them I'm struggling, what stories will they write about me? What will they believe—not about what I'm capable of, but about who I am?

And here's what happens. The more we say those things to ourselves, the better we get at saying them. The more convincing they sound. And the better we are at not asking for help, the more the people around us assume we've got it all together—capable, talented, handling hard things with ease. They never stop to check what's actually happening behind closed doors in our minds, our hearts, our bodies.

And the cycle of not asking continues.

Sound familiar?

Here's the problem.

If anyone came to us with those excuses for why *they* weren't asking for help, we'd be beside ourselves.

Imagine your best friend telling you, "I didn't want to ask for help because I was afraid of what you'd think of me." Or a teammate saying, "I didn't ask for help on the project because I didn't want to let you down." We'd tell them—nonsense. You're my best friend. You're my teammate. We're in this together. There's nothing you could say or ask that would make me think less of you.

Now imagine a kid. Stuck. Facing the consequence of something they couldn't handle alone. And when their dad finally asks why they didn't say anything, the kid says, "I'm sorry. I didn't want to bother you. I thought I should be able to do it on my own."

We would never allow the people we love to give those excuses for not asking us for help. So why do we give those excuses? Why do we hold ourselves to a standard we would never hold anyone we care about to?

I think it's because the more we succeed, the higher we climb, the more we buy the lie that *leadership is lonely*.

It's a phrase I've heard for most of my adult life. The idea is that the buck has to stop somewhere, and where the buck stops is a lonely place. I have sympathy for that. I understand it. But for most of us, that's not the truth of our lives. Leadership doesn't mean we have to do life alone. It only feels that way when we refuse to ask the people around us for help—the people who care for us, who love us, who would drive to Taco Bell at noon or answer the phone at 11:15 on a Tuesday night without a second thought.

The loneliness of leadership isn't the absence of people.

It's the consequence of refusing to ask the people who are there for help.

■ ■ ■

Here's the thing about believing leadership is lonely: It's a vicious cycle. The better you get, the more people give you. The more they give you, the more you have to figure out on your own. The more you figure out on your own, the higher people think of you. The higher they think of you, the more they give you.

The cycle goes on and on.

And somewhere inside it—whether we're living the cycle ourselves or watching someone else live it—a belief begins to take hold.

Asking for help means something is wrong with me.

We see other people handling more than we are without missing a beat and we think, *What's wrong with me that I need help to do less than they're doing without it?* We struggle to keep up with the pace, the demands, the expectations—and we unconsciously assume that because the expectations exist, we must be able to meet them without help. And we wonder, quietly, *What's wrong with me?*

This question doesn't come to life the same way in everyone, but they all lead to the same place.

■ ■ ■

Have you ever seen the photo of Atlas holding the world?

In Greek mythology, Atlas was a titan who fought against the Olympian gods and lost. As punishment for his rebellion, he was sentenced to stand at the edge of the world and hold up the heavens forever. Over time, that sentence came to be depicted a different way: as a man holding the weight of the entire world on his shoulders.

It's the weight of responsibility.

And it starts out feeling like we're doing something good for people who can't do it for themselves. And over time, as the pressure builds, the thought of letting your family down—of taking one wrong step—becomes unbearable. When people see how much you can hold, how strong you are, they give you more and more to carry. And over time, a quiet belief starts to take hold: *If I ask for help, maybe that means I'm not strong enough to carry all of this.*

This is not a weight born of pride or laziness. It's a weight born of responsibility and the unexamined belief that when I take on responsibility, I give up the right to ask for help.

I see this posture often.

I see it in athletes who are the first in their family to make it big: the first to go to college, the first to play at the next level, the first to earn real money. The weight they're carrying isn't just their own performance. It's the hope of everyone who came before them and everyone who is counting on them now.

And I see it in parents who grew up with very little and now, as adults leading their own families, have found success—and have taken on the weight of making sure their kids have more than they had. Every opportunity. Every resource. Every door open that was closed to them. The determination that all the traumas that shaped them will not be passed down to their kids. That's a beautiful burden. And it's a heavy one.

The longer we carry a weight like that alone, the heavier it gets. Heavier because more responsibility keeps getting added. Heavier because the cost of failing gets higher the longer we've been holding. Heavier because we get tired, and we refuse to let the people closest to us down. We reject the idea that we couldn't—or wouldn't—pay whatever the cost is.

Because underneath all of it is the thing we will not say out loud: *I'm terrified that I might not be strong enough to endure.*

We plant our feet and we hold. And for a while, it works. The weight is heavy, but we can carry it. The people who love us don't know what's happening, but they see our strength from the outside, and we let them see what they see.

But the longer we carry the weight in silence, the more fertile the ground becomes for something to grow in it. Something we never intended to plant: resentment.

*You don't appreciate me. You don't see how much I'm doing. How dare you ask for more?*

That's the devolution. Responsibility is the reason we start holding. But when we refuse to ask for help, responsibility doesn't stay responsibility. It grows roots in the soil of our silence and becomes resentment toward the very people we thought we were carrying the weight for.

The longer we refuse to ask for help, the more susceptible we become to the poison that grows when help is never asked for.

■ ■ ■

Other times we have trouble asking for help because we have trouble trusting people. Consider the following teaching story.

Kay was on her way. She had moved through the ranks faster than anyone around her, and she was humble about it: gave credit to her team, passed the fruits of her success on to others. She was the kind of leader people wanted to follow, not because she demanded it, but because she made the people around her better. She asked for help when she needed it. She trusted the people closest to her. And it was working.

She was even willing to be open and vulnerable. One night, out with friends, she shared her insecurities about the next position she was rumored to be promoted to. Nothing alarming. Nothing disqualifying. Just the natural fears that come with taking on something new.

The next week, someone else got the job.

Later she found out that one of those friends—someone she had trusted with the quiet, unpolished version of herself—had been jealous of her success and leaked her insecurities to their boss. Not as what they were. As something worse.

Kay vowed to never make that mistake again.

*Been there. Done that. Never again.*

Kay didn't build walls. She didn't make a dramatic exit from the community. She just asked for a little less. Relied on others a little less and on herself a little more. She looked for confirmations that people would let her down, and she found them everywhere—a disappointment here, a broken promise there, an unmet expectation that proved what she already believed.

*If I want it done right, I'll do it myself.*

That became her script. Her armor. The phrases she repeated until they stopped feeling like protection and started feeling like truth.

Every relationship that disappointed her got written off. Every category of person who burned her got excluded. Her world kept getting smaller—not because people abandoned her, but because she stopped letting anyone in.

Ever felt that way?

The scary part is when you are right about people enough times that you start to feel vindicated in your narrowing. Every new disappointment confirmed the belief. Every time someone fell through, you think, *I was right to pull back*. But what we don't see is that when you filter for disappointment, or look for confirmation that people couldn't be trusted, you will keep finding it—where you focus you finish.

The cost isn't loneliness exactly. The cost is being right in a way that protects the very belief that's killing you. We build a fortress that keeps hurt out, and miss that the same walls keep help out, too.

■ ■ ■

There is one more posture that keeps us from asking for help, and it doesn't come from responsibility turned to resentment or hurt turned to distrust. It comes from watching. And assuming.

We watch the leaders above us, the people around us, and those ahead of us. And it seems like everyone has it all figured out. They seem to know the answers. They seem to handle things with ease. And without realizing it, we start building a list. A rubric. An unwritten standard assembled one observation at a time.

The first time it clicked for me that I was grading myself on a scale that made no sense was my senior year of high school.

Throughout early high school, Bret Page was the guy I looked up to. In all the ways I had learned to measure what mattered, he was crushing it. He took the time to invest in me, and a kind of mentor relationship was born. I did my best to follow in his steps. I worked the summer job he worked. I lifted like he lifted. I filled the leadership positions he vacated. I wanted to be him. But no matter how hard I tried, or what I accomplished, I never felt like I imagined Bret to be.

Then one summer, Bret came back from college—he'd earned all-conference honors as a linebacker—and after we finished working out, he made a comment that I was bigger than he was.

It didn't register.

I didn't feel like I was bigger than him. How could I be? He was Bret Page. But "bigger than" is not an opinion. It was a fact. But the facts didn't cut through my rubric of what it meant to be Bret Page.

Can you relate?

Maybe you don't have a Bret Page. But you have an algorithm that feeds you a constant stream of what your life should look like, what you should be doing, and—most damaging of all—how nothing you do can compare to the curated lives of everyone else in the world. The rubric has never been easier to build. And it has never been harder to meet.

Your boss never seems stressed. Add that to the list. Your mentor always has the answer. Add that to the list. That mom on Instagram has it all together. Add that to the list.

The list grows. It's never written down, examined, or questioned. It just accumulates—silently, unconsciously—until it becomes the standard we measure ourselves against.

You have to know all the answers.
You can't have bad days.
You can't make mistakes.
You have to do it all.
And whatever you do, you can't ask for help.

Nowhere has someone mandated these rules. You never consciously picked these expectations up, but you feel the weight of them every day.

Here's what's so cruel about this. Whatever is on your unexamined list—you can't meet every expectation on it. Nobody could. But because every other leader you watched seemed to meet it, you conclude the problem is you. Not the list. You.

The leader carrying this doesn't feel burdened the way Atlas does. This leader feels deficient. Like everyone else got a manual they didn't get. Like everyone else is pulling it off and they're the only one faking it.

And the cruelest part: The people they were watching are doing the exact same thing. Building their own impossible lists from watching other people. Performing competence for an audience of people who are performing competence. Nobody asked for help because nobody saw anyone else asking for help. A feedback loop of silent assumptions.

And even if we were doing better than the people we looked up to, we wouldn't feel it. We'd think it should be easier. *I should be more patient. I should have figured this out quicker, better, with less struggle.* Because no matter how well we do, we never feel like we live up to the imaginary rubric.

The cost of this posture isn't exhaustion or a shrinking world. It's believing you're the only one who can't get it right—and never checking, because checking would mean admitting you don't have it figured out, which is the one thing the rubric says you can't do.

■ ■ ■

Now here's the problem with all three of these postures.

We get really good at them.

We adapt. We optimize. We tough it out, get stronger, use it as motivation, and find a way to reach our goals. For a while. But no matter how smart, strong, or stubborn you are, the cost of living inside these patterns will catch up to you.

You can carry more weight than me. You can go further alone than me. You can push yourself to more extreme limits than I ever will. But it's kind of like having a long-jump contest across the Grand Canyon. You might jump farther than me. You might look more impressive in the air. But we're both going to hit rock bottom.

That's the consequence of doing life alone. Of never asking for help. Of carrying weight we were never meant to carry alone. Of never examining our beliefs.

But what if it didn't have to be this way?

## The Uncommon Belief

**I don't have to do it alone.** Independence is not strength. Asking for help is not a sign that something is wrong with me—it's how I show my strength.

---

You are not a superhero. You don't have superpowers forged in the fires of another planet or laboratory. You are human. You have limitations. And one of those limitations is that you can't do everything alone.

Even the Lone Ranger had a sidekick.

That's not to say there is no value in an independent spirit—the kind that is willing to strike out, take a risk, or move first. I love that spirit. The problem arises when that spirit becomes a stance. A posture. When independence becomes isolation.

When your independence causes you to look down on others because they need help—that's a problem.

When your independence forbids you from asking for help when you genuinely need it—or would even just like it—that's a problem.

When your independence forces you to take on more than you can handle in a healthy way—that's a problem.

So what's the alternative?

It's to believe that we don't have to do it alone. That my strength is found in and through the strength of others. That there is an interdependency that moves me further than I could ever go on my own.

Is it harder? Sometimes.

Does it have its risks? Everything does.

But is it worth it? Absolutely.

■ ■ ■

I've lifted weights since I was 12 years old. Every max lift I have ever set had two things: Metallica cranked up to 13 and a spotter.

Why? Because a spotter does five really important things:

- A spotter makes sure you are in the right position to succeed.
- A spotter encourages you as you push yourself to your limits.
- A spotter makes sure you don't get stuck under a load you can't lift.
- A spotter encourages you to try things you would never try alone.
- A spotter celebrates with you when you succeed and encourages you when you miss.

If you don't have a spotter, it is next to impossible to actually max out. You may lift more than you have before, but it isn't a max—because you know that if you miss, you need a way out. That mental block holds you back. Forces you to leave something in the tank. Just in case.

Isn't it interesting that when we have a spotter, we don't call ourselves weak or discount our work. Why is that? Because we already know—in the weight room at least—that to be your best, to hit your max, you will be as strong as you are willing to ask for help.

Who are you willing to ask for help?

## The Four Relationships Everyone Needs

You don't have to be a weightlifter to have a spotter in your life.

You don't have to be on a team to have teammates.

What we all need—however you describe the role—are people we are in relationship with. People we can ask for help. People who can ask us. If we're going to do the uncommon thing and live life with other people, we have to answer one question: *What are the relationships I need in my life?*

There are four.

### Relationship with Yourself

The first relationship you need is a relationship with yourself.

You have to be right with you.

That sounds funny to say, but here's what I want you to see:

If you don't know yourself, you won't know where to ask for help.

If you don't have self-confidence, it will be hard to be humble enough to ask for help.

If you can't trust yourself to do the hard work, it will be hard to trust anyone else to do it with you.

You have to be able to see yourself clearly and appreciate what you see, or you'll spend your energy trying to hide it.

That doesn't mean I need you to start talking to yourself in the third person, à la Dwayne "The Rock" Johnson. It does mean you have to take care of yourself—mentally, emotionally, and physically—so that you can receive the truth the Cycle reveals and be ready to ask for help where you need it.

**The Daily Seven** I rely on what I call *the Daily Seven*, a list of seven habits to keep me grounded, balanced, and ready to give my best. This list helps me remember one thing: *I can't give what I don't have*.

- **Faith.** Spend intentional time grounding yourself in what matters most. It's not about how much time—it's about showing up with intention.
- **Physical.** Take care of your body. You can't afford to ignore your health.

- **Spouse (or loved ones).** Connect with your spouse or the people closest to you. Laugh together, dream together, remind yourselves why your relationship matters.
- **Kids (or friends).** Be intentional about connecting. When life gets busy, don't put your most important relationships on the back burner.
- **Service.** Do something kind for someone else with no expectation of reward. Service keeps us grounded, reminds us of our purpose, and is an antidote to entitlement.
- **Personal.** Do something just for you. A cup of pour-over coffee instead of something quick. A book that makes you laugh. Small moments that refuel your soul.
- **Work.** Focus on today's work. Make a list. Tackle it. Move on. You can't do it all, but you can do what's in front of you.

These specific practices may be for you, or they may not. The point is the same: Before you can be your best, before you can ask for help, you have to be right with yourself. Find how you do that. Find what builds trust with yourself, helps you see yourself clearly, and gives you the confidence to ask.

## Someone to Pour into You

What do the best athletes, musicians, actors, and leaders all have in common?

They all have a coach.

You need one, too. A coach, a mentor, or someone who is just a few steps ahead of you in life. Someone you can go to and ask questions such as these:

"Have you ever been in a situation like this?"

"I'm about to take on this new project—what don't I know that I should?"

"How do I do this?"

They aren't babysitting. They aren't there to hold your hand. They are there to show you how to grow. To help you up when you get knocked down. To give you perspective you can't get on your own.

Bill Gerkey did that for me.

Bill was an elder in our church, and one Sunday he asked how I was. I told him, "Mr. Bill, I don't know if me and my son are both going to survive to his next birthday."

He said, "So, your boy is doing his job?"

I was confused. I was under the impression my son's job was to do whatever I told him to do.

Sensing this, he continued. "A young boy's job is to push his dad to his limits, so the dad can learn what it means to truly love unconditionally."

Some part of me knew this. But no other dad I hung around with said that out loud. How could we? We were in the thick of it.

A few weeks later, Bill asked me, "How's our boy doing?"

"Mr. Bill," I smiled, "he's employee of the month."

**Building Your Coaching Staff** This relationship is not theoretical. You actually have to have people and places you can turn to for help. Whatever area you want to grow in—life, leadership, marriage, work—you need a coach. You can't grow without one. And you need to name them *before* you need to call them.

Who are the people you turn to for different layers of support?

Sue Enquist calls them her *board of directors*. My friend Stephanie Dillard—volleyball coach turned high school principal—calls them her *Mount Rushmore of Influence*. I call them my *coaching staff*. Whatever you call them, here are the roles they need to play:

Inspire you to a higher level of character and performance

Teach you new skills

Challenge you personally

Hold you accountable

Know and love the real you

Some of these roles can be filled by people you'll never meet in person—coaches who reach you through books, podcasts, and other teaching. Sometimes you have one person for each role. Other times, one person fills all five. The point isn't to check boxes. The point is to be intentional about finding the people you need to help you take your next step—whatever it is.

## Someone to Walk with You

There's an African proverb: If you want to go fast, go alone. If you want to go far, go together.

Cliché or not, it teaches a powerful truth. We need people to run beside us in the ultramarathon that is life.

This is someone in the same age and stage as you. Someone walking through the same challenges. Someone who can understand what it's like to be in your shoes *right now*.

This is the person who can not only speak truth to your doubts but also can empathize with your struggle in real time. Mentors have already been where you are—they have advice from the other side. But they're on the other side. Sometimes the most powerful encouragement isn't the encouragement born of past experience, but of *shared* experience. You can turn to them and say, "This really stinks." And they say, "Yeah, it does. Let's keep going."

My coauthor on *The Locker Room*, Damon West, and I encourage each other this way. Very few people know what it's like to spend your life on the road as a speaker.

It sounds glamorous—and don't misunderstand me, it is great—but there are more challenges than you'd see at first glance. So Damon and I play a game. Whenever one of us is grinding through a delayed flight, or sitting in an airport at 3:45 a.m., one of us will text the other: "Everybody wants to be a speaker . . ."

It's our way of reminding each other: "Yeah, this is hard. But it isn't bad. We aren't the victims. It's a gift to do what we do."

And it lights a fire in me every time.

**Building Strong Relationships** Relationships like this don't just happen overnight. They're built over time on the foundation of trust. And trust takes time.

Remember: You can't make old friends. But you can build new ones.

To do that, you have to get to know people. What makes them laugh? What are their interests outside of work? What's their family life like? What's the foundation of their life? These are just a few questions to start with. Here are a few ways to build the relationships:

**Spend time together.** Especially with the electronics put away. Bonus: Eating a meal together is the best way to spend time. BBQ accelerates the rate of relationship growth—trust me.

**Remember things about them.** Their birthday is a great date to remember. What's better is remembering they don't like anything orange-flavored, or that their younger brother has a chronic illness. The details matter. Take notes if you have to.

**Keep your promises.** If you say you'll do something, do it. It's that simple.

**Seek their input.** People like to feel needed. When you humble yourself enough to ask for help, you show them you trust them—which makes them want to trust you back.

**Admit your mistakes.** Everyone makes them. Mistakes can be forgiven, but only after they're admitted. When you admit yours, you signal that you can be trusted to take responsibility next time, too.

There are countless ways to build strong relationships with people at your age and stage. However you do it, the point is simple: *We need someone to walk with us, or we will burn out.*

## Someone to Pour Into

The last relationship you need is someone you can pour into.

Or, in the language of this chapter, someone you ask to let you practice giving help.

Think of it like this. There are three kinds of people in the world. Doers. Achievers. Leaders.

**Doers** do what needs to be done to stay where they are. They're satisfied with what they have, and they're happy to let their world revolve around their three favorite people: me, myself, and I.

**Achievers** achieve to get ahead. This one is tricky, because it can sound like this is the goal. But the problem is that an achiever's end game is *getting themselves* ahead. They may practice uncommon discipline. They may even hold uncommon beliefs. But they're using them as fuel to propel themselves forward.

**Leaders** lead to help others get ahead. They recognize—as we'll see in Chapter 11—that the purpose of leadership is to help other people. It's not about me. Which means that if I have knowledge, skills, time, resources, or ability, and I don't share them with someone else, I am at best an achiever.

I can't cross the bridge to become a leader until I start pouring into someone else.

And here's the great news: You don't need a title or even talent to be a leader. You just have to be willing to serve someone. One of my favorite teachings from Martin Luther King Jr. comes from his sermon, "The Drum Major Instinct":

> *Everybody can be great, because everybody can serve. You don't have to have a college degree to serve. You don't have to make your subject and your verb agree to serve. You don't have to know about Plato and Aristotle to serve. You don't have to know Einstein's theory of relativity to serve. You don't have to know the second theory of thermodynamics in physics to serve. You only need a heart full of grace, a soul generated by love.*[1]

When was the last time you helped someone like that?

■ ■ ■

I started this chapter by asking, "When was the last time you helped someone?"

I'll close this chapter by asking, "When was the last time you let someone help you?"

That's a harder question to answer. It's easier to give help than it is to ask for it.

When you refuse to ask for help, you are not protecting others from burden, or proving how strong or responsible you are.

You are denying the people who love you the thing they most want to give.

Help.

You know this—because you'd answer the late-night text without hesitation. You don't call the person on the other end weak for sending it; you call them brave.

Real strength isn't found in never needing help, but in being strong enough to ask for it when you do.

## The Pressure Test

What do you need help with that you haven't asked for help with?

The thing you've been holding for weeks, months, maybe years—the one nobody knows the actual size of, because you've carefully curated how people experience your struggle.

Now ask yourself why you haven't asked for help?

Be specific. Not *I don't want to be a burden*. The real reason. The story underneath the struggle. The one that, if you said it out loud, might sound like one of these:

*If I ask, I have to admit I'm not who I've been telling everyone I am.*

*If I ask, I'm proving the thing I've been trying not to be: weak, struggling, behind, deficient.*

*If I ask, I lose something I can't get back. Standing. Trust. The version of me other people built their expectations on.*

*If I ask, the person on the other side might not show up the way I need them to, and I'd rather not know that than find out.*

*If I ask, I'd be giving up control of something I'm not ready to hand over.*

One of those is yours. Maybe more than one.

Now look at what you're carrying. Look at who is in your life. And answer the only question this chapter has actually been asking:

> *Who are you going to ask, and what are you going to ask them for?*

Not someday. This week.

## Note

1. Martin Luther King Jr., "The Drum Major Instinct," sermon delivered at Ebenezer Baptist Church, Atlanta, Georgia, February 4, 1968.

CHAPTER

11

# It's Not About Me

I refuse to live or lead in a tit-for-tat system—I don't keep score. I freely give the best of me to whoever is in front of me. Always.

It was one of those moments in life where you thought you were in a movie.

Everyone noticed when the Range Rover pulled up. The door swung open and out stepped a woman I can only describe as rich, powerful, and successful. She just had a look about her. When she walked in, the doors flew open. The wind blew her hair right. Everybody in the Starbucks knew somebody had just walked into the room. Everyone had that look on their face. Is she famous? Should we know her?

Her hair was done. Her nails were right. Her shoes were expensive. She had the power suit on.

And when she walked up to the counter, the young lady across from her could not have been more different. She was surely on her first or second day. She was socially awkward. She didn't have the people skills or the presence, especially compared to the woman standing across from her ordering.

The woman was direct. No nonsense. She hardly looked up from her phone as she ordered. Not at all while she waited. You had the sense that this stop was a necessary interruption in a very busy day—because it turns out that no matter how successful, driven, or intimidating you might be, we all have the same kryptonite: coffee.

What happened next is hard to believe if you weren't there. And yet it's also the most predictable thing that could have happened.

As the awkward barista brought the woman her drink, her toe must have caught the rubber mat behind the counter. She lurched forward, squeezed the drink, and launched the woman's coffee ounce by ounce through the air, in slow motion, for a direct hit on the woman's blouse.

The coffee shop went silent. The barista instantly broke down in tears. In between her sobs, she tried to clean up the mess and apologize and disappear all at the same time. The manager rushed out from the back, moving past the barista toward the woman—already bracing to do damage control with the customer.

Her ensemble, now ruined by a Frappuccino, surely cost more than that girl would make in a month. The inconvenience. The embarrassment. The day thrown off schedule. Delays that would cost her who knows how much.

She had every right to be angry. Every right to demand something—a refund, a manager, the barista's job. Every right to name the cost, out loud, in a room full of people who were waiting for her to.

She didn't.

The woman took the barista by the shoulders and said, "Look at me. Are you okay? Don't cry, honey. It's just coffee."

And then she started helping the barista clean up.

No demands. No viral Karen moment. Just a woman stained with coffee, helping clean up a mess she didn't cause—for a first-day barista who had nothing to give her in return.

■ ■ ■

I can't tell you why that woman responded the way she did, but I can tell you what it cost her.

She had every right to raise all kinds of hell. This wouldn't have even been an unreasonable moment for her to go full Karen. Her clothes were ruined. Her day was thrown off. She'd had a hot coffee poured all over her. She could have sued them and potentially made a ton of money. She had every right to lose her cool and—in that moment—to treat the barista as less than human.

But she didn't. At that moment, she chose to see the person across from her. To set aside what was rightfully hers and take care of the barista rather than her anger. She deployed compassion rather than demanding the situation be made right. She helped clean up a mess that wasn't hers, when she could have rightfully complained about how her clothes, her day, and her expectations were ruined. She accepted responsibility to serve the person in front of her.

I don't think it's a stretch to say that this was an uncommon response.

## Tit-for-Tat Accounting

I've told this story enough times to know how people react to it. And the reactions are all over the map.

Some people say, "No way—I would have gone viral in that moment, and I would have been justified." There's no way they'd have kept their cool.

Others say they would have lost it and then tried to reel it back in—the apology would have come after the outburst.

Others say, "It depends. Is this a Starbucks I go to every day, or am I just passing through? How inconvenient was the timing? Where was I headed? How much margin did I have left that morning?"

Others say they'd have gone full Daily Stoic. "It's fine. Don't worry about it. It's just coffee." And walked out a little stiffer than they came in.

And others say they'd have downplayed it in the moment but asked for some free coffee, or a gift card, to make the most of the situation—turning the spill into a small transaction.

Of all the responses I've heard, there's one I almost never hear: *"That's exactly what I would have done."*

Because what the woman did wasn't one level past the common response. It was two or three. She lapped demanding her rights. She lapped the stoic brush-off. She lapped the work-the-situation for a gift card move. And she kept going—past all of it—to actually serving the person who had just spilled coffee down the front of her suit.

■ ■ ■

I'd really like to believe that in that exact situation I would react the same.

But there are plenty of scenarios in which I know myself well enough to know that I might fall well short of that mark. On days where scarcity is really loud, my temper and patience get short. When I have a master schedule planned out down to the minute, and this Starbucks stop is already flirting with being too much of a stretch to make the next one on time. When I'm peopled-out and just want to get my coffee and fade out of the spotlight.

In those moments, I can see myself stopping at downplaying the situation with a curt "Don't worry about it" and moving straight to the logistics of reworking my day. Or playing the polite liar—outwardly telling them it's okay, while inwardly thinking the exact opposite.

I think you can relate.

If we can go cold over coffee, what happens when the stakes go up?

How do we treat someone when we're afraid that if they get theirs, there won't be enough left for us to get ours? How do we carry ourselves when we watch someone younger, less experienced, less deserving on paper rise faster than we did? How do we respond when a peer gets the recognition we thought was coming to us? Is there any room left for us to serve someone when we're that focused on protecting what we think is ours?

Nobody wakes up hoping to become a self-centered jerk. Sometimes it happens because we stop examining ourselves. Sometimes it happens because we don't have anyone in our lives who will check us. Sometimes it happens because we're so focused on doing well that we never notice the moment we start to cling.

Why does fear, comparison, jealousy, and selfish ambition all lead us to a place where we are less than generous with the people in front of us?

Tit-for-tat accounting.

You do this to me, I do that to you. If I do that for you, you have to do this for me. It's an endless system of IOUs, favors, horse trading, and transactions. Every relationship has a ledger. Every interaction is a line item. And in that system, there is no room for a response more generous than the terms.

The iPhone has a set price. You pay what it costs. If Apple wants more for it, they have to give you a newer version. If you want to pay less, you have to buy an older one. The transaction completes, the ledger closes, and everyone walks away square.

That works great in the marketplace of products.

It brings out the worst in people.

■ ■ ■

Let's play a game. I am going to present you with three scenarios. I want you to answer as honestly as you can this question: What would you do?

**Scenario 1.** You've coached this program for 12 years. Built it from a losing record into a contender. Your top assistant is 20 years younger than you, incredibly talented, and rising fast—you know the head coach opening at the bigger school across the state has her on their shortlist. You have influence. A phone call from you to the right person could put her over the top. Or you could stay quiet and let the process run its course without you, and in six months still have your best assistant on your staff.

*What do you do?*

**Scenario 2.** You were sure you were getting the director role. Everyone told you it was yours. When the announcement comes, it's someone else—a colleague you mentored for their first two years in the department, someone who knows what they know in part because of what you taught them. Now they're leading the meeting you thought you'd be leading. They find you after and want to thank you—they know they wouldn't be here without you. They want to keep learning from you.

*What do you do?*

**Scenario 3.** You are one of four candidates for a role you've wanted your whole career. The others are qualified. You are qualified. There is exactly one chair.

One of the other candidates is struggling with a high-visibility project—the kind of struggle you have helped each other through before. No one would ever know you helped. But leaving them stuck makes them look less capable. You have the answer they're missing. You know it. They don't.

*What do you do?*

■ ■ ■

If we're honest—really honest—most of us aren't sure what we'd do in those moments. Or worse, we are sure, and we don't like the answer.

In every one of those scenarios, the math is on the side of the clinging response. Don't make the call—you'll lose the assistant who makes your program work. Keep your distance—the one who got what should have been yours doesn't deserve more of your time. Stay quiet—your rival's stall is your opening.

There is a strong argument to be made for trusting the math.

The math is not wrong.

That's what makes this common belief so durable. Not that the accounting is flawed. That the accounting is accurate. When you do the math, clinging makes sense. You worked for this. You sacrificed for this. You earned this. Of course it feels justified to protect it.

Tit-for-tat accounting will produce a competent leader. It will not produce an uncommon one.

Because the uncommon move—the one the woman in Starbucks made—is not available inside the accounting system. Not because the math is wrong. The math is fine.

The uncommon leader is just not running math.

## The Uncommon Belief

**It's not about me.** I refuse to live or lead in a tit-for-tat system—I don't keep score. I freely give the best of me to whoever is in front of me. Always.

---

This belief isn't about finding different or better math.

It's about throwing the ledger out the window altogether.

Which is a completely upside down way of thinking, even in the servant leadership world.

Servant leadership calls leaders to think beyond themselves, to care for people, to invest in others. When you read Robert K. Greenleaf, the father of modern servant leadership, he presents a vision of leadership that doesn't keep score. He calls it the *best test*:

> *"Do those served grow as persons? Do they, while being served, become healthier, wiser, freer, more autonomous, more likely themselves to become servants? And, what is the effect on the least privileged in society? Will they benefit or at least not be further deprived?"*[1]

This reframes leadership around the well-being of others. But when we look at how it gets applied in business contexts, something shifts.

Almost every servant leadership teacher I have seen emphasizes service—adding value to people, putting others first, serving your teammates—and then makes a claim about what happens next.

You've heard the same lines as me:

- "Pour into your players and they'll run through walls for you."
- "The better you care for your employees, the better they will care for your customers."
- "Serve your team and they'll follow you anywhere."

The inputs are relational. The payoff is performance.

Serve your people and they'll be more loyal. Invest in them and they'll perform better. Care for them and they'll follow you further. The inputs are different. They're better. They're more human.

But the structure underneath hasn't changed. Do *this* so *that* happens.

That same pattern shows up across the broader servant leadership world. Walk into any airport bookstore and the leadership shelf will tell you the same story. *The best leaders serve their teams—and their teams win more.* The research agrees.

Study after study, book after book, points to the benefits: higher engagement, stronger culture, deeper trust, better results.

And none of that is wrong. In fact, it's often true. But look closely at the logic: Better relational inputs lead to better organizational outputs.

It's still math. It's just better math.

And that's the thing this belief rejects. *I refuse to live in a tit for tat system. I don't keep score.*

Why? Because if my serving is motivated by the results I hope to gain, even if they are a natural outcome, I'm not serving. I'm using acts of service as an input to the equation. I'm still, at some level, keeping score. I may have changed what I'm putting into the equation, but I haven't actually let go of the equation itself.

■ ■ ■

What does it mean to let go of the equation?

I'm not asking you to ignore that there are real results from serving others; I'm asking you to not be motivated by them.

It isn't giving up on outcomes—outcomes still happen.

It isn't pretending to not care—I'm asking you to care for people more, not less.

It isn't martyrdom—you're not trying to lose—you're trying to help other people win.

Letting go of the equation means not consulting it, being motivated by it, or allowing it to be the filter through which your actions are decided.

In his translation of "The Apostle Paul's letter to the Philippians," Eugene Peterson penned a line that shows this clearly:

> *"Don't push your way to the front; don't sweet-talk your way to the top. Put yourself aside, and help others get ahead. Don't be obsessed with getting your own advantage. Forget yourselves long enough to lend a helping hand."*[2]

This is the upside down way of life and leadership. It's a climb to the bottom, not the top.

I have this passage memorized. It is the heart of my ethos and teaching. I talk about it a lot. But even as I write this section, there is such a tension inside me—like my breath is catching. But seeing those words in black and white leaves no room to negotiate a win or plan for a positive personal outcome.

*Put yourself aside.*

*Help others get ahead.*

*Forget yourself.*

This is a call to serve without reserve. To look for those in need and serve them. Especially when it costs you.

■ ■ ■

One of my best friends in high school was a kid named Jerry.

When Jerry moved to town our freshman year, he was living in a foster home. He had lived in a lot of foster homes over his 15 years. Jerry was the kid who had faced more hardship, struggle, and unfair bad breaks than anyone should have to. And yet—he was full of an energy, talent, and a love for life that was contagious.

At the end of our freshman football season, we got word that Jerry was being moved to another home. We were all crushed. He had an impact on us in a real way. Including our coach.

Coach was everything you could want in a hard-nosed football coach. He coached us hard, but loved us harder. He was a man of integrity, faith, and conviction. Jerry had affected Coach, too.

So much so that Coach and his wife—both educators, with three kids under 10 at home—made the uncommon decision to adopt Jerry. To bring him into their family and raise him as their own.

We were blown away. To this day, it is one of the most impactful demonstrations of the upside down way I have ever seen. Not just because he adopted Jerry. But because he kept loving Jerry even when Jerry took advantage of him and repeatedly broke his trust. After 20 years of it, Jerry betrayed the family one last time and left for California. We've only heard rumors of where he is now. None of them are good.

When I talked to Coach about it, he told me something that is still hard for me to process:

*"Knowing everything I know now, I'd still do it again."*

The upside down way doesn't come with a guaranteed happy ending. Sometimes the joy of serving genuinely erases the sting of the cost—you pay what it takes, and the paying itself is enough. Sometimes it doesn't. Sometimes you pay, feel every bit of the cost, and the joy never shows up to balance the books.

Sometimes a return comes. The loyalty, the culture, the credit, the trust—it flows back to you, sometimes twice over. Sometimes it doesn't. Sometimes the serving is one-way, and the person you poured into walks off with what you gave them and you never see it again.

The uncommon leader pays the cost without knowing what follows it. Not because they're stoic. Not because they don't care. Because the question has stopped mattering.

■ ■ ■

So how do we do it?

How do we actually live this way—not as an idea, not as an ethic, but on a Tuesday morning—when the riptide is still pulling, when the ledger is still whispering, when the person in front of us has less and we have to decide in real time what we're going to do with the gap?

Most of us aren't Coach yet. We're on our way, or we hope we are. Which means we need practice. Two of them. One is what you do. The other is who you become.

## How to Live the Upside Down Way

### Be the Right Size

The uncommon leader learns to read the moment.

The question is never *Am I being big enough?* or *Am I being small enough?* in some abstract sense. The question is *What does this moment need, and what do I have that can meet it?* Sometimes the moment needs you to shrink: to give up the air in the room, to let someone else have the credit, to take the smaller seat at the table, to let the younger leader run the meeting. Sometimes the moment needs you to expand: to take responsibility no one else wants, to speak the hard truth no one else will, to carry weight that would crush someone less equipped.

Either move can be the right one. Either can be the wrong one. What makes the difference isn't the size of the move. It's the motive underneath it.

Ego shrinks when it wants to be noticed for being humble. Ego expands when it wants to be needed. Both are still about the leader.

The right size is what the moment needs, not what makes the leader look good, feel good, or protect something they've earned. The leader reads the room, reads the person in front of them, and spends themselves accordingly.

Coach spent 20 years being the right size for a son who broke his trust over and over.

Sometimes that meant expanding—showing up, again, to a situation no one else was willing to walk into. Sometimes it meant shrinking—absorbing a hurt without retaliating, taking a smaller role in his own home so Jerry had room to be raised. The posture shifted constantly. The discipline underneath it didn't move.

Read the moment. Spend what it needs. Don't attach to either size.

## Live with Mudita

I learned about the idea of mudita from Patrick Murphy, the head softball coach at the University of Alabama. It's a word that roughly translated means "the vicarious joy of watching someone else succeed." Not the tolerance of their success. Not the performance of being happy for them. Actual joy. The kind that rises in your chest without having to be manufactured.

Without it, every win for someone else registers, somewhere in the body, as a loss.

You can't will mudita into existence. You can't decide to feel joy for someone else's success and then feel it on command.

But you can feed it. And what feeds it is gratitude.

**Gratitude for the people who have loved you.** The memory of being loved—really loved, the costly kind, the kind that cost someone something to give—is what makes loving someone else feel less like obligation and more like echo. You don't pour into others because a leadership book told you to. You pour into them because someone poured into you, you remember what it did, and you want someone else to know that.

**Gratitude for what you have.** Everything you're holding can be taken away. Your health. Your position. Your platform. Your relationships. None of it is permanently yours. That awareness—held honestly, not morbidly—dissolves the entitlement that makes us cling. You stop protecting what you were never going to get to keep.

**Gratitude for what you've learned.** Every piece of wisdom you operate from was taught to you, whether by someone who got it right or by someone who got it wrong. You didn't invent what you know. You received it. And the leader who remembers their teachers—the ones who modeled it and the ones who cautioned by negative examples—wants to pass on what they were given. Hoarding knowledge starts to feel like a small betrayal of the people who gave it to you.

**Gratitude for your opportunities.** Yes, you earned things. Also you are standing on the shoulders of people who went before you, whose work made your work possible, whose sacrifices cleared the ground you built on. Generosity toward the people coming behind you isn't charity. It's continuity. It's passing forward what was passed to you.

When you live gratefully—when the memory of what has been given is active rather than forgotten—giving stops being an effort. It becomes the natural response to having received. The reps aren't forced. They're fueled.

This is what mudita actually is. Not a trained suppression of jealousy. A cultivated memory of grace, which produces, over time, the vicarious joy that is its natural downstream.

When someone else wins, the grateful leader doesn't have to override loss. There is no loss to override. Everything they have was a gift. Someone else receiving a gift doesn't diminish their own. It extends the thing they're grateful for.

That is when the belief becomes who you are, rather than what you're trying to do.

■ ■ ■

The upside down way does not offer a very compelling offer. Get drenched with coffee? Help clean it up. Invest in your people? Don't expect a return. Turn your life upside down to give someone what they couldn't get themselves? No fairy tale ending guaranteed.

Ready to sign up?

It is true. The upside down way can suck.

That's why not many will live this. Sure, some will use it or take advantage of it, but few will live it.

It's also true that the cost can be real. But here is what I believe: You don't serve others to win. You serve because that's what a leader does.

You lead to serve and serve to lead.

That's what it means to believe *It's not about me*.

## The Pressure Test

Think about the last time you served someone you lead.

Not a hypothetical. A real moment from this week or last. The time you stayed late for someone on your team. The time you covered for them. The time you advocated for them in a room they weren't in. The time you poured into them when nothing required it.

Now look deep in the mirror.

Were you keeping score? Not consciously. Not as a ledger you'd ever admit out loud. But somewhere underneath—was there a calculation about what this would net you? The loyalty it would earn. The reputation it would reinforce. The leader it would prove you to be.

If there was, the act was real. The cost was real. And it was still math.

That is the trap the chapter has been naming. Not selfish leadership. Generous leadership that has not yet given up the ledger. Math doesn't have to be greedy to be math.

This is the test. Not whether you serve. Whether you serve free of the math.

1. When you served someone this week, were you quietly expecting anything in return, and would you have served them the same way if you knew it would never come?
2. Where in your leadership are you running generous math and calling it servanthood?
3. If your team's growth stopped translating into your own—no recognition, no advancement, no platform, no return—would you keep pouring into them with the same intensity?
4. Are you a doer, an achiever, or a leader, and does your answer align with what the Cycle reveals?

## Notes

1. Robert K. Greenleaf. *The Servant as Leader*. Robert K. Greenleaf Publishing Center, 1970.
2. Eugene H. Peterson. *The Message: The Bible in Contemporary Language*. NavPress, 2002.

CHAPTER

# 12

# The Things I'm Proud Of

I thought writing this book would be easy.

Not because writing a book is easy, but because I'm really good at giving speeches.

I spent over a year developing, delivering, and fine-tuning the speech this book is based on. The audiences ranged from NBA players to a hospital system to business leaders, educators, and teams. I was so confident in the material, I told my publisher that I'd have the manuscript done in five months.

Tops.

My mom always told me that pride goes before a fall.

For three and half months I tried and failed at making my speech and this book align. It was like pushing two like magnets together—the harder I tried to force them, the more they resisted.

The problem was in how to get the ideas from my head to the page. When I speak, the gestures, the timing, the photo on the screen behind me—they all do work the words alone don't have to.

A speech can hide things a book can't. When I tried to put my speech on the page, I came face-to-face with all the places where my words or ideas weren't as strong as I thought, where my delivery and presence did more work than my arguments, and where I was flat out wrong.

And it sucked.

I ping-ponged from one extreme of thinking to the other.

One moment I'd write a line and say, "Ohhh! That is good!" and then the next I'd go to edit the title page and be uncertain about how I spelled my name.

This was most real when I wrote Chapter 9. The chapter on mastery, fittingly, was the one that exposed how much I needed to check my own needle.

■ ■ ■

"Babe! Babe! You gotta hear this!"

My wife looked up from her desk with genuine curiosity. I don't normally read her portions of the manuscript—I know it's going to change 17 times before it makes it to print, so I like to let her experience it without the backstage pass.

But I was so excited about the section I had just finished that I broke my own rule and interrupted her workday to share it.

I didn't just read her Chapter 9. I performed Chapter 9 for her.

When I finished, I smiled and asked, "What do you think?"

She delivered her thoughts with cold finality.

"Yeah. I don't get it."

That was not the reaction I was going for.

Instead of gushing over my brilliance, she gave me a cold-water truth: You don't have things quite as figured out as you thought.

And she was right.

I closed my laptop. I walked straight to the pantry and ate all of my kids' Oreos.

When I was done drowning my sorrows in Oreos and milk, I realized there were only three options. Ignore the reality of where I was. Fight with it. Or do the work to change it.

That's it. Three choices.

What would you choose?

■ ■ ■

The obvious answer was "Listen to your wife, Mack. Do the work. Rewrite the chapter."

Of course.

And.

I really liked the chapter I had written. I thought I was clever. I connected ideas in creative ways. I wrote some really funny jokes.

And.

I really didn't want to do that work. I wanted to be done with that chapter. I was embarrassed that the thing I thought was so good left me feeling so exposed. I hadn't felt exposed before I examined it.

I had actually felt great. I wanted to go back to that feeling.

For me, this is the place I hate being the most:

- At the crossroads of hard change and comfort
- Stuck between what you know is right and what feels good
- Intellectually clear but emotionally snuggled up in bed

Whenever I'm stuck here, it's because I know being who I said I wanted to be is about to require more of me than I planned to give.

It's not hard for me to imagine that this book has asked more of you than feels comfortable to give. One, two, or all of the uncommon beliefs we examined brought up hard truths, old hurts, things you've worked around for years.

What the Cycle revealed hit closer to home than was comfortable. The work before you is more costly and demanding than you had budgeted.

And now, Ian Morgan Cron's words land differently:

*This is life. These are its terms. What am I going to do about it?*

You can choose to ignore what this book revealed to you. Be okay with staying right where you are: Pitch a tent and stay comfortable. You can intellectually affirm and even love this book, and not change a thing about your life.

It can live on your bookshelf, stand out in your Zoom background, and signal to the world that you care enough about your character to read a book about it. And ignore the reality that you didn't care enough about your character to do anything else about it.

Second, you can choose to fight against it. Fighting usually feels pretty good—until it doesn't. The lie that fighting tells you is that you can win the argument between your comfort and what the Cycle revealed.

But the truth is undefeated.

You can argue with yourself about it. You can post online about how terrible this book is. You can write me an angry email. You can rightly point out flaws in what I wrote. But if you go that route, you will miss the one gift this book tried to give you: a mirror to see yourself more clearly.

Or, and this is the hardest, you can do the work. Not the work of biggering. Not the work of proving anything to anyone. Not the work of looking like you're doing the work.

The work of going back to the one chapter that exposed what you would rather hide from and reading it again, slowly.

The work of telling one person what the Cycle revealed, and asking them for help.

The work of changing one specific thing today, not because it's strategic, but because you have seen the person you want to be, and refuse to let another day go by living as someone you have outgrown.

■ ■ ■

The seven uncommon beliefs are not a random list of ideas. They are an intentional path that moves us, in their own way, through the Cycle.

**Hard Isn't bad** gives you the posture toward adversity.

**Optimism requires no evidence** gives you the posture toward uncertainty.

Together they answer the question: *How do I show up when the conditions are against me?* Without **hard isn't bad**, optimism becomes denial—positive thinking with no capacity to absorb the hit. Without optimism, **hard isn't bad** becomes a cheap form of stoicism—absorbing hit after hit with no conviction that the hit is worth absorbing. They need each other. One without the other is incomplete.

**I am not my performance** is the belief that the system hinges on.

If your identity is built on performance, then adversity not only brings challenges into your life, it threatens your identity, value and worth.

Uncertainty becomes an existential crisis, not a situation to deal with.

Truth becomes a verdict and mastery becomes a stopping point short of your potential.

Asking for help becomes an indictment of your inabilities, and your insecurity demands you be the center of your corner of the world.

**Truth is not my enemy** and **mastery is not the destination** together answer the question, *How do I keep growing once I've started to succeed?*

Truth keeps you honest about where you actually are. Mastery keeps you reaching past where you've already been. Without truth, growth becomes self-deception—improving without ever being challenged on whether you're improving the right thing. Without mastery, growth has a stopping point, and any belief with a stopping point eventually becomes a tent.

**I don't have to do it alone** and **it's not about me** together answer the question, *Who is this for?*

Help moves you out of isolation. Purpose moves you out of yourself. Without help, the work stays trapped inside the leader who built it—strong, but alone, and eventually too heavy to carry. Without purpose, the work serves only the person doing it, and any belief that ends with the self eventually corrodes the self.

The system produces the competitive advantage the book promises only when all seven are continually working together. Not because seven is a magic number, but because each belief helps you answer a question the previous belief cannot answer by itself.

■ ■ ■

The question driving this book is simple: *Is your character strong enough to carry you through life's hardest moments?*

Not your talent. Not your work ethic. Not your reputation or your results or your résumé.

Your character.

I believe that question deserves an honest answer and the way you find that answer is not by accumulating a pile of traits, but by examining your life with ruthless abandon.

Character isn't something you possess. It is something you practice, develop, and build.

And it can never be taken from you. That's what makes it the competitive edge that lasts.

It can, however, be given away. That's why throughout this book I've shown you not only where and how our beliefs, actions, and character fall out of alignment but also how to diagnose yourself.

As long as you are willing to do that work, the edge that is your character will never dull or fade. That work will give you the examined beliefs and deliberate behaviors needed to close the Integrity Gap between who you say you are and who your patterns reveal you to be.

■ ■ ■

When I think about the things I am most proud of in life, they are always the hard things. I don't remember the easy things. I've never thought, *Wow! That workout was so easy I'll never forget it!*

The lessons that have made the biggest impact in my life were the hardest learned lessons. The work that is my favorite often begins as the work I want to do the least. That's how I know I need to do it.

Chapter 9 was the hardest chapter I wrote. It took the longest, had the most revisions, and changed the most from what I thought it would be.

It is also my favorite.

That's not to say that it is the best chapter in the book—that's for you to decide. But it was the hardest chapter to write. It cost me the most—hours, edits, and words deleted, yes—but it forced me, more than any other, to do the work of this book. It forced me to put in the work, and then look honestly at what the Cycle revealed.

I'm proud I did that work.

What hard work are you proud of?

The hard work this book is asking of you isn't found in the 50,000 words you read. Reading the book was the easy part.

The hard work will be found on a Tuesday this summer, when 15 of those words materialize from the far reaches of your memory, hold up a mirror at the most inconvenient time, and show you a truth you don't want to see.

The work will be hard. Uncomfortable. Costly.

It will force you to reckon with the areas of your life that are out of alignment and the places that are exactly as you've built them to be. That reckoning will not be one of judgment, but of invitation. The invitation to see the truth of who you are when the pressure is on and to do something about it.

When that day comes, I wonder, What will you do?

Ignore it?

Fight it?

Or do the work?

# Acknowledgments

One of the things I am most excited about with the release of this book is the opportunity to talk to people about the concepts I teach in it.

For months, this book has been a conversation with me, myself, and I. And don't get me wrong—I love me some me—but even too much of a good thing is too much.

While this has been a solo work, I am not the only one who has paid the price of creating it. So many people have worked extra, sacrificed, and paid real costs so I could give my attention and effort to putting this book together.

First, and foremost, I want to thank my family.

My wife, Teressa, has been my biggest fan, most faithful supporter, and biggest investor in every project or hair-brained idea I have ever had. She is the one who turns down the intensity of her own brilliant work when I am putting in long hours. She is the one who solo-parents when I am on the road or glued to my computer. She is the one who has to navigate the choppy waters of my emotions when I am overwhelmed, overworked, or simply in a bad mood. No matter how much work I have put in, I can promise you she has put in more. This book—or any work I do, for that matter—wouldn't be possible without her sacrifice.

In that same spirit, I want to thank my children—Harrison, Jane, Porter, and Jack. They share their dad with the world. Every time I am on the road speaking or at the office writing, it is time I am not playing catch with them or spending time at home. They are awesome kids, and I couldn't have done this work without their willingness to share their dad with the world.

To my team at 2Words Character Development: Colton, Luke, Brandon, Windy, and Jen. All five are experts at what they do, and most of all, the kind of people championship teams are built on. Their discipline, work ethic, and trustworthiness allow me to focus on the things only I can do. Most of all, though, they are my dear friends. Thank you.

To the team at Wiley Publishing—Shannon Vargo, Zachary Schisgal, Amanda Pyne—and the many others who work behind the scenes. Thank you for believing in me, and for trusting me to rightly handle the incredible reputation of Wiley.

And finally, to my parents, David and Mary Mackey. They will never get to hold this book in their hands or read this acknowledgment, but I know that if it weren't for them, I wouldn't be who I am today. Their sacrifices, their love, and their uncommon beliefs laid the foundation for the man I am today. I hope this book, and my life, honor them well.

—Stephen Mackey
Blanco, Texas
Spring 2026

# About the Author

**Stephen Mackey** is a *Wall Street Journal*–best-selling author, keynote speaker, and one of the nation's most trusted voices on character and leadership development. His message is simple and uncommon: Championship people win championships.

A proud first-generation college graduate and Texas public school product, Mackey earned his BS from Texas A&M University and a master of divinity from Fuller Theological Seminary. In 2017, he launched 2Words Character Development with a simple goal: *What would it take to help one million athletes and coaches connect the dots between sports and life?*

Today, 2Words has reached more than 2.5 million students and coaches in over 30 states and is used by over half of all public schools in Texas—making it one of the largest leadership and character programs in the country.

In 2024, sportsmanship in the state of Texas was out of control. This led Mackey to create The Texas Way, a first-of-its-kind statewide sportsmanship initiative that produced a 13% decrease in student ejections, a 12% decrease in coach ejections, and a 28% decrease in fan ejections, after only one year.

Since 2017, Mackey has delivered more than 1,700 speeches to students, educators, coaches, and business leaders across the nation.

Mackey serves as the leadership development coach for the Texas High School Coaches Association—the largest coaches' association in the world—and as the character and leadership coach for Formula Zero, the leadership initiative founded by 9× NBA All-Star Damian Lillard. He bridges the worlds of education, athletics, business, and public service with a message that connects across generations.

Mackey lives in a small town in Texas with his wife, Teressa, their four kids—Harrison, Jane, Porter, and Jack—and their mini-goldendoodle, Lucy.

# Index

*Claude Sonnet 4.6 and Opus 4.7 by Anthropic were used as a developmental editor and conversation partner throughout the writing of this book. Specifically, I used Claude to test my arguments, challenge structure, and sharpen my thinking. The ideas, stories, and conclusions in these pages are mine, and every word was written or rewritten by me. I take full responsibility for the content of this work.*